THREADS OF GRACE

SAY YES QUICKLY BOOKS

7715 East Highland Avenue
Scottsdale, Arizona 85251 USA

Copyright © 2024 by Eliza Richards.
All rights reserved.

Cover photograph by Kevin Gent / Unsplash.

ISBN 979-8-9898660-1-4

First print edition.

THREADS OF GRACE

A Mother's Memoir of Love & Addiction

Eliza Richards

Say Yes Quickly Books

For Alexander and Robin, with a lifetime of love

*No matter how dark the tapestry God weaves for us,
there is always a thread of grace.*

An Old Hebrew Saying

Author's Note

To help protect my family's privacy—and also widely share this story—I have changed my name, the names of my two sons and their families, and the names of my former husband and his wife. Everyone else's names are accurate. To the best of my ability, so too are all the events I describe—the weave of darkness and the threads of grace.

The Shooting

My son Robin was on my mind; he was almost always on my mind. But this was different. Something was wrong with him. I felt it. But I couldn't find him. I had tried for several days in that summer of 2008 to reach him in rural northern California where he lived, but he never picked up his phone.

A few times in the past I had hired detectives to look for Robin, but this time was different. Lewis Martinez, a detective I had worked with before, hadn't been able to find out anything. Robin *might* be down in the Central Valley town of Visalia, and he *might* be in the hospital there. But other than sharing that possibility with me, he said he really couldn't help.

I called Mark Smith, a physician I knew who the head of emergency services at the Washington Hospital Center, to see if he could make some calls to find out if Robin was in the hospital in Visalia. But because of HIPAA privacy laws, Mark was told by the people he spoke with at Visalia's Kaweah Health Medical Center that they couldn't say if Robin was a patient there, let alone what condition he was in if he *was* a patient.

When Mark called to tell me he had struck out, he said the only way I could find out about Robin's condition would be to fly out there myself. I was in my early 70s; I had COPD and long flights weren't easy, but I couldn't just sit and hope that Robin—or someone—would call to tell me he was okay.

So, on July 25, I got on a plane and made an eight-hour, one-stop flight to Fresno and a fifty-mile taxi trip to the Visalia hospital. I told the lady at the reception desk that I was there to see my son Robin Fleming, and that I understood privacy laws and I wanted to speak with the head of the hospital. She told me to take a seat in a waiting area, so I sat for what seemed like a very long time. Eventually, I was approached by a man who introduced himself as Steven Kennedy, a detective sergeant with the Visalia police department.

He inspected every piece of identification I could produce, then told me that Robin *was* a patient at the hospital. He had been shot in the heart, liver, and lung and was in extremely serious condition. Robin had been taken to the emergency entrance to the hospital in a pickup truck and left there to get inside on his own. He made it inside before he collapsed and was rushed into surgery, where three surgeons worked side by side to perform a sternotomy, an exploratory laparotomy, repair of the right ventricle of his heart, the bullet wound to his right lung, extensive liver damage, and pack and wash his interior abdominal cavity. The surgeons had not expected him to live, so when they finished the surgery, they draped him with sterile towels instead of closing the massive incision in his chest because it seemed likely that they would have to go in again if his condition worsened.

As we sat in waiting-room chairs, Detective Kennedy told me the Visalia police had no idea who shot Robin or who drove him to the hospital. Then he led me through a long labyrinth of corridors to an isolated and dimly lit room where Robin was lying in bed. I don't know why, but while I was traveling I had stopped at a pawn shop—a place I had never been to before—and bought a small gold locket with the last lines of an anonymous poem called "Footsteps in the Sand" engraved on it. The poet asks God why, in some of the most difficult times of his life when God had promised to be with him, he saw only one set of footprints trailing behind him in the sand. God replies: *My precious child, I love you and will never leave you. Never, ever, during your trials and testings. When you saw only one set of footprints, it was then that I carried you.*

I pinned the locket to a light sea-green mohair throw that for many years I have kept at the foot of my bed at home; it was something both boys had liked since they were young and a small comfort from home. I covered Robin with the blanket—the words attached to it with a safety pin. Just then, he opened his eyes and saw me. I told him I loved him, told him to go back to sleep, and said I would come back.

When I left the room, Kennedy was waiting outside, and he walked me back to the hospital entrance. When he asked where I'd be staying, I told him I thought I would stay at the motel I'd seen that was adjacent to the hospital, and he walked there with me, he pointed out a restaurant across the street where I could eat while I was in town. He was very pleasant and seemed genuinely concerned about my welfare. It never crossed my mind that at that moment the detective was taking charge of me to be sure that I wasn't in danger myself. Later I realized that he was afraid the shooter might want to kill me, too.

After dinner, I went back to the hospital and walked again through the maze of hallways to Robin's room. I found him sleeping quietly, the mohair throw still draped over him. I was careful not to wake him. The next day, I spent all day at the hospital, although Robin slept most of the time. He would occasionally wake up for a moment or two. I was terrified that he would die—die alone—so I didn't want to leave him. But I did go back to the motel each night for several nights in a row. Then I flew home to Washington and went back to work, Robin's condition slowly stabilizing although he was still in terrible pain.

I returned to Visalia two weeks later. This time I rented a car and I brought with me a book, *Water for Elephants*, which I had enjoyed and thought Robin would, too, when he was well enough to read. When I saw him at the hospital this time, not only was he well enough to read, but he could also sit up in bed, carry on a conversation, and he had been visited by two friends.

The next day, I met with Dr. Han Soo Kim—the principal surgeon who had operated on Robin. Dr. Kim seemed to be a kind and gentle man. He told me that it had been an "all hands" effort to save Robin's life. They had nearly lost him several times while he was on the operating table, but he neither he nor Detective Kennedy could tell me anything about the shooting. And Robin made no comment. He said he had never before seen the guy who shot him, and he certainly didn't know why he had been shot, nor did he know who had driven him to the hospital and why he or she had rushed away. I didn't believe any of that.

Since he was an adolescent, Robin had been a drug user. He had been a heroin addict for at least two decades. He worked for years in California's illegal marijuana trade in far-northern Humboldt County. Why had he gone down to the Central Valley? Was the shooting part of a heroin deal gone bad? Was it simply one of the many risks of the often-dangerous marijuana trade? Robin wouldn't say. As far as Detective Kennedy and his colleagues were concerned, Robin was simply the victim of an attempted murder. And Robin continued to say he knew nothing at all that could help them piece together what had happened.

When I went back to the hospital on a Sunday morning, Robin had been moved to a new room, and I had to search to find him. It finally dawned on me that the police and hospital officials were moving him from room to room constantly to keep him safe, and that *I* was under police protection, too. When I told Kennedy that I planned to drive up into the hills to see the place where Robin was shot, Kennedy told me emphatically that I would *not* be doing that. He made it crystal clear that he would approve what hotel rooms I stayed in, which restaurants and stores I visited, and when I could travel in my rented car. I realized that the police were concerned for my safety as well as Robin's, and I should do whatever they said.

On Tuesday, Detective Kennedy returned to the hospital with Duane Cornett, a lieutenant in the police department's violent crimes unit. Robin listened as they told him they were convinced he *did* know who shot him. They explained as they pressed him hard that they were conducting an attempted murder investigation and that his help would be essential. But Robin could not—or would not—help them.

Detective Kennedy told me privately that Robin was about to be released from the hospital and that he had made arrangements for Robin and me to stay in a suite at a Holiday Inn near Fresno's airport before flying to Washington. I thanked him and told him that would be nice because I could swim at the hotel pool. He said that swimming was absolutely out of the question. I would not be safe out in the open and neither could I leave Robin alone. The shooter might be waiting for a good moment to finish the job he started and make it certain that Robin could never identify him.

I was in Robin's hospital room when a woman named Chrissy came to visit. She was blonde and a little over-weight, the wife or girlfriend of Robin's friend D.J. D.J. had visited the hospital earlier, alone, but this time Chrissy came in his place. She brought Robin tea from Starbucks and cheerfully told me about her three children and her parents, who ran pack trips in Sequoia National Park. She offered to lend me her pass so I could drive into the park free of charge. But soon, Robin angrily accused me of being rude to Chrissy, claiming that I had grilled her for information she did not have, so I left in a huff.

Late that afternoon, Robin was discharged. He was extremely thin and unsteady. He shook uncontrollably and a liver drainage tube still protruded from his abdomen. He apologized for what he had said to me earlier. I gave him the clothes I had brought for him, and we talked about whether he actually was well enough to travel back to Washington with me. Because he was so unsteady, it was a struggle to get him into my rental car. At the pharmacy where I attempted to fill the prescriptions he had been given, I was told the pharmacy would need Robin's physicians' verbal confirmation that they had indeed prescribed what I assumed were controlled narcotics. I panicked. It was closing time, and the doctors were leaving the hospital. Robin was shaking badly and looked ready to faint. I frantically tracked down one of the surgeons, who then spoke with the pharmacist and signed off on the drugs.

At the Holiday Inn, I wasn't sure I could get Robin to our suite. But walking very slowly we made it. I opened the door to a narrow hall that led to a small sitting room with a fold-out sofa where I could sleep. A second short hallway led to the bedroom where I immediately put Robin to bed. I gave him his medications, then went to the restaurant to get food for both of us. He ate just a bit before he fell into a deep sleep.

That evening, I telephoned Maisie Maquire, a friend on the women's board at the Washington Hospital Center. I told her that Robin would be flying with me to Washington the next day and that I had no idea what condition he would be in. I asked her to arrange for someone at the hospital to see him immediately on our arrival. Maisie said she would do what she could and that she would call back. When she did, I was shocked by what I heard. "It's time for a little truth-telling here," she said. "Robin is indigent, and the hospital doesn't want any more indigent patients." I couldn't believe my ears. I felt like my blood was on fire. For one thing, Robin was *not* indigent—and neither was I. I couldn't imagine that anyone in his extreme circumstance could simply be turned away but, according to Maisie, that was the final word.

On Wednesday morning, Robin seemed a little better. I packed our few things and his medications, and we set out for the Fresno airport. Driving into the sun, I had trouble reading the highway's big green signs and responding to their directions, and Robin was alarmed. "Mom, you can't see!" he shouted—and he was right—so he did the navigating, and I did my best to drive. Detective Kennedy called to say he was traveling with Detective Cornett in a car with lights and sirens trying to reach us before our plane took off. They had photographs of suspects they wanted to show Robin in hopes that he might identify the shooter. They got to the gate just as we were about to board, but Robin told them he didn't recognize anyone in their photos.

During the long flight across the country, the flight attendants did everything they could to keep Robin comfortable, and I was grateful, but several times when I looked at him and saw how frail and ill he was, I was afraid he would die in-flight. When we landed and he was still alive, I called Joel Guiterman. He was my own long-term physician and he told me to bring Robin in. He and Robin spoke about what had happened in California; Joel said the liver drain needed to be changed—and soon. Tressie, his nurse, attempted to draw blood for testing, but she could not find a vein. After decades of shooting heroin, his veins had collapsed, so they sent him to a lab down the street where a trained phlebotomist would draw the blood. But the people at the lab couldn't find a vein either, so when we returned to Joel's office, he told Robin to go alone into a nearby room and draw the blood himself—which he did. Robin was a pro, after all, at finding veins with a needle.

Over the subsequent stretch of days, it was clear that I could be most helpful by making sure Robin got as much rest as possible, and that he was eating well and gaining weight—he was down thirty-plus pounds by now—and making sure he got the best possible medical care. Every day we took short walks to try to help him regain some strength—at first only around my apartment, then just a block outside, and ultimately a trip to the Bishop's Garden at the National Cathedral, a lovely, peaceful, and contemplative place he had always loved. We walked together there for fifteen or twenty minutes or until his strength gave out.

At the suggestion of Joel Guiterman, I took Robin to the emergency room at George Washington University Hospital at two o'clock in the morning—at a time when Joel said it would be less crowded, Robin would get immediate attention. People at the hospital did see Robin right away and took him into surgery because his liver drainage tube urgently needed to be replaced. That surgery went well, and by late afternoon the following day he was released. He was weak and very tired, but I managed to get him home and fed him before he dropped off to sleep.

I was still working, so I had spent the morning hours at my office at 13th and I streets. Robin was nervous whenever I went out, so I always told him I would be home by 1:00 p.m. But I made sure to get home by noon or close to it so he wouldn't worry. One day I arranged for us to meet Jim Mayer, a leader of Wounded Warriors. Robin and I walked to a nearby Starbucks, where we met Jim, a man who had lost both legs in Vietnam. He told us how he often would go to Walter Reed Hospital, walk into the room of a veteran who had just lost a limb and ask, "Hey, soldier, you want a milkshake?" He was known as "The Milkshake Man," and the milkshakes, he said, invariably led to conversations—good ones, important ones, and he believed his hours with those soldiers helped them prepare for lives that would be very much worth living. Robin listened carefully, but he said little, and he was totally exhausted by the time we walked the three blocks home.

The following day, I called him from the office and asked him to walk to my bank to get some cash—another trip of just three blocks each way. When I got home, he had made the trip, but he was white as a sheet and was sweating and shaking uncontrollably. I realized that what was different about this outing was that it was the first time since he had been shot that he was out in the world alone—and it terrified him. He was afraid that he would be shot again, and I hadn't realized till then how very vulnerable he felt. He was almost forty-years old and had survived jail and a horrific injury to his right foot and the challenges of a junkie's life out on the street and up in the California hills, but this time someone had tried to kill him. I did my best to calm him that afternoon, and I assured him that he was safe—although, of course, I didn't *know*, in fact, if he was.

I continued to send him out on short errands by himself to help build his strength and sense of security. He spent several days with his father and stepmother Jenny at their farm near Lexington, Virginia, and I made an appointment for him with a psychiatrist named Carlotta (Buffy) Miles, with whom Robin met several times during September and October, talking with her about the trauma of being shot and almost dying. Of course, he didn't share their conversations with me, but I knew Buffy was helpful.

On October 24, Dr. Juliet Lee, whom Robin had been seeing for a month or so, removed the tube that had been draining his liver and gave him prescriptions for methadone, hydrocodone, and some other powerful opioids.

Later that day, he announced that it was time for him to go back to California. He said that California was where he lived, where the people closest to him were—it was the place where he wanted to be. I told him I would much prefer for him to stay longer, but I wouldn't stand in his way. He had gotten much healthier in recent weeks. He had put on weight and gained confidence, and I had little choice, although seemed certain to me that he would be returning to extremely dangerous circumstances on the West Coast.

On Tuesday, October 28, he asked me if I would drive him to the airport. I said no. Doing that would have seemed to approve his decision, which I didn't. He was leaving—that was clear—so I offered to drive him to the George Washington University Metro station, where he could get a train to National Airport.

I pulled over at the intersection of I and 23rd streets to let him out. He got out of the car, took the small bag that held his stuff and said goodbye. He walked a few steps away. Then he stopped, turned, and came back to the car. He got into the passenger seated and turned to me and said, "Thank you, Mom, for saving my life." I cried all the way home.

From jail in California sixteen years before, Robin had written a long poem whose first lines were *Stone walls do not a prison make/Nor iron bars a cage/But heroin has locked me up/And turned me to a slave.* For two decades, I had been the mother of a heroin addict. Both my sons, quite separately, had become addicted to heroin as they were growing from adolescence into adulthood. Robin's older brother, Alexander, had gone to Hazelden in Minnesota and got clean and sober there. He now leads one of the nation's most successful addiction-recovery programs, and lives with his wife and family in St. Paul. But Robin—irrepressible, charismatic, and quick-witted Robin—was an addict still, one whose life was in shambles. I never knew when I saw him if it would be the last time.

I did understand by then that Robin could not be helped until *he* chose a new life, until *he* chose to get sober. But somehow I could not just abandon him to his addiction and his decades of bad decisions. He was my son, and I couldn't turn my back on him. A mother's love never dies. I had worked hard in business and earned my way, but I could never shake my fear that I was a failure as a mother—the worst kind of failure a woman could be. Had I really helped Robin? Was he correct? In the months since the shooting, I had done what any mother would do. It wasn't much. But Robin's last words to me as he left for California and a sure descent back into his hellish life meant more to me than anything.

John

When I met John Fleming in 1963, I thought he was the most handsome man I had ever laid eyes on. My family lived in Washington, D.C.—I was an army brat from a family with a long and distinguished military background. There was something about John that simply bowled me over. We were both distant descendants of Francis Scott Key, and that's how we met. He was tall; he had broad shoulders and narrow hips and ice-blue eyes. I took one look and thought, I'm going to marry that guy.

An army man until he retired, my father, Wilfrid Mason Blunt, was a West Point graduate, a cavalry officer, an avid horseman and polo player. He was a bit colorful for an army man, with his jackets from Huntsman in London, yellow socks, and silk handkerchiefs, and he was old enough that he had been an officer in World War I. When I was a young girl, he was the commanding officer of Fort Carson, just south of Colorado Springs. We first lived in a house on Cascade Avenue in town and moved to a small house on the grounds of the s Broadmoor Hotel at the foot of Cheyenne Mountain. My world was focused on horses and ice skating. My father had let me choose my own horse and was mortified when I named him Socks. I kept him in a stable across the street from our house, and in winter I skated in the Broadmoor Ice Palace for hours every day.

I once heard my parents say they were afraid I would grow up thinking all the world was that idyllic, but I knew what a lucky little girl I was. Although I was not the brightest of the three siblings, I knew what I liked and what I didn't like. My sister Ellen's idea of a good Christmas present may have been a wildly expensive dictionary, but my idea of a great present was a cashmere sweater.

When we moved to Washington after my father's retirement, my parents enrolled me in a Catholic girls' school with cloistered nuns in Bethesda. The school and I were not a perfect fit. I was used to almost total freedom and required almost no discipline. I got up early to skate, kept my own schedule, took care of my horse, and generally didn't cause any trouble. I just didn't learn multiplication or much of anything else. I couldn't play sports in my new school because I had to be tutored for math, tutored for reading, tutored for everything. And I remember the headmistress, calling me into her office and telling me she knew how smart I was and what an excellent student I would be if only I would try harder and apply myself.

One day, one of the nuns took me aside and told me she knew for a fact that I was "possessed by the devil." Really? The school's academics didn't give me *time* to be possessed by anything, as far as I was concerned. And I decided that the nun just made that up to push me to work harder. For many years, I had done far more skating and riding than schoolwork and had to make up what I had missed academically. I had some attributes and was probably smart enough, but the rigid rules at the Catholic girls' school were hard for me to accept. I did love the learning—especially English literature and poetry taught by Mother Benoit, and I stayed in touch with her for many years. She instilled in me a lifelong love of reading. And I did make friendships with the girls in my small class of fifteen.

After high school, I wanted freedom. I wanted to go to a co-ed school where I could meet boys and have fun. I spent a couple of years doing just that at the University of Maryland—until my father gave up on trying to educate me.

It was early in the 1960s when I went with my family to a meeting of Francis Scott Key's descendants to discuss whether to form a society in his honor. John was there with his mother. I was working at CARE, the international relief agency, and I remember one of my co-workers there telling me that John Fleming was *not* marriage material, but I wasn't interested in the slightest in that advice. I was going to marry him no matter what anyone thought.

John called one day and said, "Put on your diamonds and let's go to a dance." We did and we began to see each other often.. In my opinion, he was a far better catch than any of the Kennedys. He was stunningly handsome, totally charming, and he was as drawn to me as I was to him. In addition to being the most gorgeous man I had ever seen, he came from an old military family like mine. He had an elegant education—St. Paul's School, Princeton, and the University of Virginia law school. He worked at AID—the Agency for International Development—and his father had been with the state department. He lived in a tiny apartment in Georgetown, where, I assumed, the two of us would live once we were married.

He was thirty-four; I was twenty-eight, and the Cuban Missile Crisis and President Kennedy's very recent assassination made us feel we should grab life and run with it. My father, retired Colonel Wilfrid Blunt, did not want me to marry John. I went to see an old family friend to ask if she knew why Daddy didn't like him. She said my father's father had been a soldier of fortune—a rake—who abandoned his wife and child. He was known to drive around the Philippines in a horse-drawn carriage, wearing a white suit. She said he had ice-blue eyes just like John and was the spitting image of him. My father just couldn't look at John without seeing his father.

Although John's family background and mine were similar, our lives at home were very different. My mother was sweet and charming. She wrote a poem for every occasion and made all her children's friends feel welcome. Alice Fleming was a lawyer. She lived in a house full of antiques with silk upholstery and had a spaniel named Judge who sat on her lap. She had her chair and John had his. When we got engaged and I went to meet her, I realized that I was the *only* person John had ever brought home, male or female. Alice and I got along, but in a rather cool sort of way. She gave us a lovely engagement party, and I think she was just relieved that John was going to settle down.

My family was Catholic, and John's was Episcopalian, so my parents decided the wedding would be at the Chapel at Arlington—neutral territory and a beautiful and very military kind of place. I wore a dress that came from the evening gown department at Garfinckel's. It was made of very heavy jersey, designed by Malcolm Starr, a couture designer in those days. My sister Ellen was my sole attendant, and she wore a long yellow silk dress also made by Starr. The chapel was packed, and when John and I left it had begun to snow. He helped me down the snow-dusted steps and I looked at him and there were those ice-blue eyes again and I as happy as I could be.

Our reception was at the Army and Navy Club near the White House. I danced with my father, and I danced with John, and everyone had a great time. Before it got too late, John and I took a cab to an airport hotel where we spent the night before we got a plane the next morning and flew to the Virgin Islands and set out to sail through the Caribbean for several weeks.

Winter was worlds away from us as we sailed in the islands, and we had a lovely time in the beginning. In St. Lucia, we wandered down to the marina one evening and admired a beautiful sailboat. Onboard was a black island man wearing khaki shorts, and a big black belt that held a knife. We talked with him and discovered that the boat, the *Finnisterre*, was owned by Carlton Michell, a famous international sailor for whom the island man had sailed for many years. I asked if the boat was available for charter, and he said yes, as long as he captained it, so that was that. Off we sailed the next day. We had exactly nothing to do but enjoy the sun and the water and the exquisite islands. It was idyllic. We went where we wanted when we wanted. We fished; we swam; we napped in the sun, and John and I agreed that we would make love on every island we came to, no matter how small. But one day John got very cross; I couldn't imagine why, and when I asked he said I had to know what it was. I told him I didn't have a clue, and finally he accused me of flirting with the captain.

Flirting? I was *not* flirting with him I protested—and I wasn't. I was in love with John. It was the first time I had seen him angry, the first time I'd seen him act like a spoiled child. I couldn't know that day that he soon would prove to be a very different man than the person I thought I knew.

Throughout our honeymoon, John had told me I should call the CARE office when we reached the next port and say that I was quitting my job. I would laugh each time and tell him no. I had to give notice and do things the right way. The people I worked with were important to me. John would simply roll his eyes in mock disgust and let the subject drop until he raised it the next time. And what he chose not to tell me then was that he had already quit *his* job. Nor did he tell me that on the day we married, he had inherited a fortune from his grandmother.

When I developed a painful cyst, a doctor on a small island was immediately concerned. He explained that the cyst could rupture and cause a serious infection. He told us we had to go back to Washington and get me to a hospital there, so we sailed to Barbados, where we caught a flight back home.

I got well once we were home in Washington, but John developed strange new behavior. He didn't want us to go to his apartment, even for a night or two. Luckily, my sister Ellen found us a house, but it was a short lease so soon we had to move again. In between houses, we slept in the bedroom of our friend Frank Seidner's apartment while Frank slept in the living room. That lasted about a week, only until a real estate agent named Corona Hayden took us to see a house in Georgetown—an old farmhouse on Prospect Street that sat at the top of a hill and had a small pool in back. But John wouldn't say how much we could afford, so I was in the dark. He did agree to drive over to the house with us, but he didn't get out of the car to take a look at the place. When Corona and I returned, I told him I liked the house and she told him what it would cost each month and he said, "Fine, we'll take it."

Life in the farmhouse on Prospect Street was like something out of a F. Scott Fitzgerald story. My job was history now—as was John's—so we would get up each morning and have a leisurely breakfast, read the papers and mountains of books till we went out for lunch. We would have a bottle of wine with lunch, then come home, have a nap, maybe take a swim, then a couple of bourbons while we decided we would make for dinner. Finally, we would have a nightcap before we went to bed. Then we would repeat that schedule the following day.

Often, we had guests for dinner and maybe a swim. Sometimes, my parents would join us; sometimes John's mother would come up from Coconut Grove to visit. While we were living on Prospect Street, my sister Ellen developed Bell's palsy, which partially paralyzed her face for a time. She came to stay with us for a few weeks while she recovered, then returned to New York, where she was diagnosed with breast cancer and had an emergency mastectomy. I heard about the emergency surgery by phone and was not able to get to the hospital quickly enough to be with her. I called my old friend Teddy Robinson, a radiologist at Columbia. He dropped everything to get St. Luke's Hospital so he could be there when she came out of surgery and could explain to her what had been done. It was an extraordinary act of friendship that I will never forget.

I think John would have been happy to continue that lifestyle forever if two more unexpected things hadn't happened. The first was that the owners of the Prospect Street farmhouse came back. We tried to buy the house, but they decided they wanted to live there again themselves. However, Barney

Patterson, a friend who owned Georgetown Properties, was able to find us another farmhouse over on 28th Street, one that we liked every bit as much, and we were able to buy it. And then I got pregnant.

I had not been in a rush to have babies and was annoyed when John's mother suggested that I see a fertility specialist she knew in Boston. It had simply taken a while. Alexander was born on August 10, 1969. For some unknown reason, John had been terrified that I would lose the baby. He thought gardening would cause a miscarriage. I was strong and very healthy, and I gardened and played a lot of tennis and felt great, but John worried. Yet that didn't mean that *he* stood up and shouldered any of the household work. It seemed to me that he simply and silently decided to do *nothing at all*. He didn't work in the garden and didn't take out the trash or do cleaning of any kind. Caring for a baby was clearly something no man should every attend to, as far as he was concerned. It was unthinkable that he would ever change Alexander's diaper—something he felt should occur, if it had to at all, in complete privacy. The one time I changed the baby while we were on an airplane, I thought John was going to jump out of the window rather than suffer the embarrassment.

I suspect it was a kind of embarrassment, too, that led to one of his most unusual new habits. We were in the midst of renovating the farmhouse—transforming the kitchen into a modern one and adding a deck outside with French doors that opened onto it from the living room. With the workmen who were doing the house renovation arriving early each morning, John must have been uncomfortable with the prospect of sitting in the dining room reading the newspapers while they went to work on the construction. So, he began to come down for breakfast dressed in a pin-striped suit; he would read over a long, leisurely breakfast, then would "go downtown"—wherever that was—and not return until the workday was done. I knew he hadn't found a job, but I had no idea where he spent the day, and he never said.

And if John wanted to do little in the way of making a life, he wanted me to do even less. Before Alexander was born, he was utterly opposed to the idea of my going to school. It was out of the question. He said no to the Spanish-language classes I wanted to take, and no to cooking classes. I *could* join the Women's Democratic Club and the Georgetown Garden Club, if those memberships did not become too time-consuming. Then, when I suggested that we join the Chevy Chase Club because of all the sports and activities the club offered children, he said, "You don't want to associate with *those* people, do you?" Well, yes, I thought they were fine.

John withheld any and all financial information from me, and he was baffled by why I might want to know anything. He was generous and gave me a large monthly allowance to spend on whatever I wanted with no questions asked, but if I asked about monetary details, his response was always that I couldn't understand because they involved complex "financial planning." John refused to tell me how much he had inherited—I simply never knew. We could travel around the world and stay in the best hotels and eat in the finest restaurants, that much was certain. He paid the bills he chose to pay; others went unpaid for years. He pretended everything was fine; I pretended all was well, and certainly some of the deterioration of our relationship was my fault. By not insisting that he get counseling, get a job, help around the house, or explain *our* finances, I played a big part in creating the kind of marriage that looked good on the outside, but lacked substance.

Although John had grudgingly agreed to the renovation of the house, he basically disapproved of it. He knew about fine furniture, china, and art; he had a true appreciation of things. But he wanted nothing for our house. His objections had nothing to do with cost. Early on, he said the two chairs we had were plenty. What more did we need?

He eventually relented and in the midst of our renovation of the farmhouse, I visited the shop of an interior decorator I knew and was struck by a painting I saw there. The male subject of the painting looked like John. I told him he should see it and he agreed. He thought it was his father, in fact—a man whom John had never known because he died before he was born. John became utterly convinced that the painting's subject was his father. The large painting was expensive, but he decided to buy it—and *burn* it. I couldn't understand why. In the end, John determined that the subject of the painting was not his father, so he didn't buy it—or destroy it.

Robin was born on May 3, 1971, eighteen months after Alexander. My pregnancy with Alexander had been trouble free. I just got stronger and stronger. Pregnancy with Robin was far more complex medically, and so was John's attitude toward becoming a father for the second time. John liked the *idea* of fatherhood, but he simply ignored the exhausting demands of parenting one little boy—and I couldn't imagine what would be in store for us, for *me*, once there were two very young children in the house.

One evening during my second pregnancy, John's close friend from St. Paul's, Peter Hopkinson and his wife Natasha, came over for dinner. After I served the meal, I began to feel ill and excused myself and went up to bed. Sometime in the night, I had a nightmare. People were out on the streets turning over cars, blocking streets with them, and heaving them onto front lawns. When I woke up, I found that something similar to the events of my dream had actually happened right outside our house. The May Day protests against the war in Vietnam created chaos throughout the city and more than 12,000 rioters were ultimately arrested.

That morning, I called Dr. William McKelway, my obstetrician, to see if he would come see me—something OBs actually did in those days—he said he wasn't sure he could get to me because of the rioting, and that the best thing to do would be to go the hospital because at least there would be people there who could take care of me. John and I made our way to George Washington Hospital, and I remember the television showing live footage of the riots. Meanwhile, the medical people who were taking care of me became increasingly concerned. When Dr. McKelway finally arrived, I asked him to tell me what was going on. He explained that he and his colleagues were worried because they couldn't detect the baby's heartbeat. It was potentially a very serious situation.

John was frantic, and the obstetrician's concern was palpable, but for whatever reason I thought everything was fine. And it was. Throughout the city, protestors against the war continued to defy the police in every way they could. I've often remembered over the years that Robin was born in turmoil and have wondered whether the circumstances of his birth played a part in his spending much of his life in turmoil as well. But at that moment, at least, he was healthy, and he soon proved to be very different from his older brother—rambunctious, unpredictable, irrepressible, and constantly in a whirl.

As time went on, the boys' father became increasingly moody and disconnected. He would sometimes lie in bed for days but say nothing was wrong and refuse to see a doctor. The bills piled up, but he simply kept them in a drawer. We had Bea, a wonderful maid and nanny. We had tons of food and wine delivered from Neam's Market, and we entertained and traveled in style. On the surface, our lives were perfect. John had been eccentric from the beginning but as years passed without work or volunteering or having anything constructive to do, he became increasingly morose, remote, and irresponsible. For my part—and it *was* a part—I never fully confronted the problems. I did love him and always hoped the cloud would lift. I think now that if I had been insistent and had forced a showdown, he might have changed. Sadly, I think I played a serious role in the disintegration of the marriage.

When Peter and Natasha held a party for Robin and their son, who was Robin's age, I was shocked when Natasha told me that out in the garden Robin had just bitten another child. I told John I thought we should take him and leave. John said, "Well, tough titties. Robin can do what he wants."

Incensed, I asked John if he would at least keep an eye on Robin. I went into the living room and sat down to try to control my anger. But soon, Natasha flew into the room and told me that I *had* to get John and Robin and get out. Robin had bitten a child a *second* time. She said Peter had angrily told John to take his son and "Leave, *now*." With that, John punched his old friend and decked him.

On the short walk home, I was in a fury. I told John that I would leave him the following day unless he agreed for the two us to begin marriage counseling with a psychiatrist immediately. Robin was just two and unaware of what John and I were talking about; Alexander wasn't with us; he was playing at a friend's house. And John said okay. But when we met with a psychiatrist, Alex Halperin, soon thereafter, John did all the talking. He told Dr. Halperin we were there because I had a complaint about him. *I* was the one with the problem and *I* was the one who needed the counseling, not him, and he was just trying as best he could to deal with my hysteria.

Alex explained that he really couldn't treat us as a couple under those circumstances but said he could treat me because I was open to treatment and wanted help. I began to go to a group therapy session led by him. Everyone in the group became convinced that the marriage to John existed in name only—and they told me so.

It couldn't have been many weeks later when I finally decided that I was going to leave. When I told John, we were upstairs in my dressing room in the farmhouse. "I'm leaving," I said, and a millisecond later John put his fist through the wall next to my head. "You can't leave. I love you," he said.

"That's not a declaration of love. That's your hand knocking a hole in the wall, and you just missed my head."

He may have loved me, but more than that, he did not want me to leave him. Yet it was far too late to stay. I had heard that a few rooms above Scheele's Market at the corner of 29th Street and Dumbarton were available, and the boys and I could take them. Although I had no idea how I could afford fifty dollars a month rent, I said I would take the little apartment. I left all the furniture, jewelry, clothes, toys, everything, behind. I took nothing except the boys. We were on our own, Alexander and Robin and me. When all was said and done, I did still love John. I just couldn't live like that with children.

Above the Market

Overnight, we had gone from seemingly having all the money in the world to having nothing at all. But at least we had a roof over our heads and for the rest of the time the boys were growing up, it was easy to explain where we lived. Home was the tiny apartment over Scheele's Market, a small corner grocery that had been a Georgetown institution for decades and was a place everyone knew. We felt safe and secure there. A quart of milk or a dozen eggs was always close at hand, and we were still in the neighborhood where the boys had lived since they were born.

In the beginning, there was no money for *anything*. With the help of friends, we acquired furniture, lamps, rugs, beds—all kind of things. Ellen Kurzman, an architect who lived across the street, made a table out of white-painted planks and two iron I-beams. It was perfect, so I copied her and made two more—one for the kitchen and one for the dining room. I bought second-hand clothes from the thrift shop that were just fine. I even found a couture evening dress for fifteen dollars. Welfare checks helped us in the beginning, and in the cold months I kept the temperature low to keep the utility bill as low as possible. I do not remember exactly how I acquired an old car but before too long I had one.

We may have been short of worldly goods, but we didn't think of ourselves as "poor." We were in far better control of our lives than before. Our telephone and heat were never cut off, and I felt much more secure. I couldn't afford much, but I could—and did—pay the bills. That was very satisfying.

My sister Ellen died on December 23. I went up to New York to make arrangements to have her body brought home and to speak with the dear friend who loved her and had looked after her. We met in her apartment, and while I was there, I got a call from Washington telling me that my mother was in the hospital and not expected to live. I had to return immediately.

From the airport, I went straight to George Washington Hospital and was able to see my mother and thank her for my life and everything she had done for me. I carried the two teddy bears the boys had sent to Ellen in New York to help keep her company while she was sick. After I kissed my mother goodbye, I went outside. It was bitter cold, the wind was blowing, and there were no taxis, so I walked all the way home with the stuffed bears under my arms—solemn and sad and cold.

The next day, the boys and I went to a Christmas Eve children's service and the priest asked all the young people present to come to the altar rail and leave their mittens for poor children in the city who otherwise wouldn't receive anything for Christmas. I was silently outraged—I couldn't believe this priest's lack of awareness that some kids at the service might actually need what they wore. I whispered to Alexander and Robin that they would be keeping *their* mittens before we slipped out.

But in that way that things have of working out, when we got home Fred Scheele and Buster and Billy—the Scheele's two employees—came by after the store closed at eight with gifts for the boys. I had a bottle of bourbon—and really nothing else to offer our Christmas Eve visitors—so we adults sat in the kitchen for a while passing the bottle around.

That was the start of a new tradition. Every Christmas Eve thereafter the boys and I hosted what became known as the Scheele Party—just the Scheele brothers and Buster and Billy and the three of us. A few others joined us over time—even a local cop who was always kind and helped me find parking spaces rather than give me tickets. The boys and I made cucumber sandwiches for our guests in later years, but the party remained a simple, meaningful event for all of us. A *Washington Post* reporter somehow heard about the Scheele Party and wanted to join us and write about it for his paper. We thanked him for his interest but said it was a very small affair, one that wasn't suited to be written about in the paper.

After the party every year, the boys and I would open the sleeper sofa and curl up to watch *A Christmas Carol* on television. We never went out on Christmas Eve because that was "the night we stay home to wait for the Baby to come," and I was happy with my sons on those Christmas Eves in our little place above the store. The following day, I would always cook a big turkey and invite a crowd—there were often ten or twelve of us—and it was quite a production to haul enough chairs up the stairs to seat everyone. But it seemed to be the place where friends were happy to be on Christmas Day.

I wrote articles for real-estate magazines about houses that were on the market as a way to bring in extra income. It wasn't literature, or even excellent reportage. One place I wrote about was South River Farm near Annapolis. A couple of families I knew owned it jointly and wanted to sell it, so I suggested writing a piece that might help:

> As I walked over its fields and wooded hills, the beauty and variety of South River Farm's trees, wildflowers, and birds struck a lasting impression. . . . South River Farm is suitable for use as a luxury estate serving two or three families; a corporate or ambassadorial retreat; a conference center; an ecological or recreational park, or, in the future when sewage facilities permit, developed residential estates.

After I found a job, I also wrote a piece for the *Washington Post*'s "Personal Glimpses of Washington" section about our unusual circumstances. The piece began:

> It's hot and I'm walking to work from my home over Scheele's Market in Georgetown. Two blocks from home my sandal breaks. Life is a series of rearrangements, after a ten-year marriage that ended in divorce. I have learned that much. Starting out again, stopping at Lorna's for coffee. She controls the informal network that operates among a few Georgetown families, swapping children's clothes and shoes when they are outgrown. I tell Lorna my boys need more tennis shoes for camp. . . . I bump into Robin, 8, rushing out of Scheele's in the brief nylon bathing suit he rarely takes off, looking guilty—clutching chocolates. What tale did he tell to get past the Scheeles? (I wish they would sell spinach cookies!) . . . George Scheele phones me: Robin was late for the bus and missed his ride to camp. I suggest Robin go down the street to Rose Park where children from a variety of backgrounds play under the strict supervision of Big Ron and Mrs. Woods, whose authority is accepted without question. Mrs. Woods once told a boy who behaved badly to leave the park and she sent him to my house when his parents couldn't be reached. She knew that if I wasn't there,

the Scheeles would be. Big Ron's specialty is field sports, but one day I found him gently tucking red tissue paper into a costume for Alexander, 9, who was to be a tomato in the local parade. . . . [At work], the usual phone calls until, "This is the camp calling. Alexander has had a riding accident." Please, God, not his head. They say it's his ankle, so I relax for a minute until I remember that my car is in the shop. A friend lends me his car for the rescue. . . . We can't find shoes to fit over Alexander's swollen ankle. He digs out bedroom slippers and is ready to go. The boys have their daily argument on the front steps, shouting for me. I'm upstairs in my underwear and can't come out. I shout out the window for them to cool it or they will disturb the peace. I skip lunch to appear at the Naturalization office on behalf of Minoo, an Iranian friend. Only in America would an Irish Catholic and a German Jew stand up together for a Muslim from Iran who wants to join us in citizenship.

The article was titled, "*Life's Rearrangements,*" and reading it again reminds me that those earliest years as a single mom were a blur of activity, punctuated regularly by terror, with George or Fred Scheele or Buster or Billy saving the day. Life was simply what it was, and not even once did I reconsider my decision to leave John. And he made the wisdom of my decision very clear every time he came around.

John and I got along no better living apart than we did when we lived together. He presumed that he was welcome inside our apartment just because Alexander and Robin were his sons—and that drove me nuts. When Alexander needed math tutoring early in his school career, John announced that he would do the tutoring—at *my* kitchen table in the evenings when I was trying to get our dinner ready. He couldn't understand why that plan was utterly unacceptable to me.

I finally had to explain to him that if he crossed the threshold of our front door, I would call the police, and to that he paid attention. He thought that rule gave him license to scream for the boys—really scream—from the street when he arrived every other weekend to pick them up for their scheduled time with him. If John happened to see *me* on the street, he would run after me and try to catch me, screaming at me just as he did at the boys unless I ducked into Scheele's, where one of them would put me in the meat locker and close the door and tell John they hadn't seen me.

Those experiences were upsetting but they were nothing compared to the discovery that John had let a whole year of bills—including those from the boys' pediatrician—go unpaid, or that he had later failed to pay their school tuition. I found it maddening, not only because as far as I knew he had money, but also because the boys didn't know or understand, and I felt it would be damaging to them for me to paint them such an irresponsible picture of their father.

It troubled me that all the discipline and parental restraint fell to me, while John was the *fun* parent, the parent who would let them do exactly as these pleased during the few hours he spent with them every month. When I came to pick them up at John's one day, I found the boys digging in the garden—not with garden tools but with Tiffany silverware bearing his family's crest.

The two boys couldn't have been more different from each other. Both were bright, but if Alexander was calm, bookish, and measured about things, even when he was little, his younger brother was something of a cyclone. I didn't talk down to them, and I included them in my adult activities. They liked that. Alexander appreciated being referred to as "my esteemed colleague" by a neighbor who had come for dinner one night. But Robin was unimpressed by that sort of thing. When another fellow suggested to him that he could grow up to be president of the United States, Robin simply said, "Well, that would be nice."

Even when he was little, Robin could leave a roomful of people he had just met and all of them would be sure he was their newfound friend. He was engaging and likeable, but he was also a hurricane.

The parents of Robin's friend Billy Trimble always rolled up their Oriental rugs when Robin came to play—just to be safe. They loved him but worried that "something was going to happen." Robin has his own ideas about things.

He didn't like to wear underwear, for example. One day, when I suggested that he should wear underwear on a visit to his pediatrician because the doctor might tell him to take off his pants, Robin's matter-of-fact response was "maybe so but maybe he won't."

The summer after John and I split, he took the boys to visit his mother at her house at York, Maine. He telephoned me back in Washington with the news that Robin was in the hospital. He had come down with spinal meningitis and doctors said he might not last the day. I was terrified. My friend Alex Halperin, the psychiatrist, was kind enough to drop what he was doing and drive me to the airport. I got a flight to Portsmouth, New Hampshire and a taxi took me the rest of the way to York Hospital. I told the woman at the desk my name and that I was there to see my son Robin. She responded that she was sorry but "visiting hours are over for the day."

I could feel myself growing physically bigger and I told her very plainly, "It is visiting hours now." What I meant was, "Either take me to my son, or I am going to kill you." She took me to Robin's room, where I found him curled up in a crib.

We were fortunate that John got Robin medical attention when he did, and Robin recovered remarkably quickly—likely from viral meningitis, the doctors believed.

It was impossible not to remember that summer illness as Robin grew older. He was the same happy and exuberant little boy he had always been, rushing to see me when I got home and jumping into my lap to tell me the day's news. In kindergarten and the early grades, his teachers all described him as likeable and engaging but said he had difficulty concentrating and struggled with fine motor skills like handwriting or cutting designs with scissors. If he got stuck on a task, he would often just stop and say, "I can't do this," rather than continue to try.

Robin was twelve when he wrote an essay for school, which he titled "Winning Is Everything," that focused on his competitive relationship with his older brother:

My brother, Alex, always treated me as an enemy and someone to beat. I tried to fight back, but it was useless. He was bigger, older, and stronger. Alex used to jump at the chance to tease and abuse me. I would usually cower and call for help, but sometimes, I would manage to defend myself. Alex, and two of his friends, Will and Frank, would often go bike riding on summer afternoons. Sometimes I was invited. They had planned to go riding one Sunday, and much to my brother's discontent, I was included. We had been riding around the basketball court in the park when we discovered a small sidewalk that ran abreast [of] a staircase running up from the court to the fieldhouse. This little sidewalk ended about halfway down the staircase with a four-foot drop. We climbed the staircase with our bikes. We sat at the top, looking over the drop estimating how far and how fast we would have to throw ourselves to make the jump intact. Andy, Will, and Frank all took the drop several times before they realized I was still just sitting there. They called me a wimp and told me just how easy it was, but still, I wouldn't try it. It was about six, time to go home, when they decided to head back, so I decided it was then or never. As I hit the jump everything went into slow motion. I saw the ground moving toward me, the rocks in the dirt looked incredibly sharp. I regretted having gone riding that day. Nevertheless, I eventually learned to jump it right, and my scrapes and cuts healed. I was proud. My brother hadn't beaten me.

I'm not sure how the biking story proved that winning was everything, but it did show that Robin was very unhappy when his brother could do things he couldn't, even though his brother was a year and a half older. The two boys argued a lot and occasionally they had physical fights. Robin always seemed concerned about whether he had his brother's approval. He needed reassurance that he was capable, successful, and a "leader." In an essay composed a few years later, he wrote:

> I consider myself to be self-sufficient, yet I work well with other people, and I enjoy school. Last July, I kayaked the Cheat River in West Virginia with Andy Bridge, a world class kayaker who

competed in the 1980 World Whitewater Championships, and several friends. The Cheat River is one of the most difficult courses in my part of the county [and] had only been paddled by one of our group previously, Andy. Andy asked me to lead as soon as we hit the river. We paddled about fifteen miles the first day [and] spent the night underneath a bridge and ate Doritos in picante sauce for breakfast.

On the second day, we covered another ten miles to the take-out spot where Andy hitched a ride back to the bus and returned to pick us up. This trip proved that I could live well with my friends for a prolonged length of time, and I distinguished myself as a leader.

Robin's expressive skills were remarkably good. He could write well for his age, and he was learning successfully at school and developing social skills—as a leader and as a follower. But long before the kayaking trip, Robin had begun coming home from school crying almost every day, asking me, "Why don't people like me?"

I was devastated. It was awful, and Robin's troubles, I feared, were likely to get worse.

The Boys at School

Robin began first grade at the Beauvoir School, the elementary school linked to the Washington National Cathedral and the Cathedral School for Girls and St. Alban's School for Boys. It was a rather snobby primary school, one his brother Alexander already attended. The boys' father agreed to pay their tuition.

Minoo Hanovar, a wonderful Iranian girl who helped me with the children, lived with us over Scheele's Market in those days. She did not pay rent and I didn't pay her. Our agreement was my promise to help her get a green card and official residence in the United States—which we eventually did get.

As they headed off to Beauvoir each school-day morning, both boys looked handsome in their school clothes, and I remember Robin rushing to me when I returned home from work to tell me the day's news from school. He was happy there and his teachers reported that he seemed to make friends easily.

Then, over time, Robin's teachers at Beauvoir began to discuss with me his difficulties concentrating. They also described problems with fine-motor skills like writing and using scissors to cut out designs. It wasn't long after that his experience at Beauvoir began to go from happy to disastrous. Classmates started ridiculing him about living over the store and not having money. He didn't understand why they treated him this way and often went to sleep in tears.

For Robin's birthday in May near the end of his second school year, he wanted to have a party and invite several classmates. I called Sarah Galbraith, the mother of one of his fellow first graders and she told me she would "have to canvas the other mothers." She reported back a few days' later that the mothers' consensus was that they would *not* send their children to a party for Robin. I was shocked and hurt. I couldn't believe that such meanness existed anywhere in the world, let alone among the parents of first graders at a church-run school.

I made up some reason for why we couldn't have a birthday party for him like we had planned, but somehow he knew the real reason. Perhaps he heard it himself from his classmates. One evening while I was giving him a bath, he began to cry and asked , "Why doesn't anyone like me?" I was crushed. It was awful. Somehow, however, we made it to the end of the school year, his final year at Beauvoir..

The following autumn, I enrolled Robin in the Maret School, which had an excellent reputation. As had happened at Beauvoir, his teachers at Maret noted Robin's inability to concentrate, but his experience there was much more positive than it had been at Beauvoir. It was during Robin's years at Maret that he became an accomplished kayaker, thanks to his teacher Nick Markoff, who ran a summer camp on the Potomac River outside the city. But Maret also allowed its students to dress as they pleased and many kids—Robin among them—took up the "Goth" style, wearing clothes that were uniformly black, black combat boots, and belts and chains and other accessories that featured metal spikes. I did my best to keep Robin in ordinary clothes, but his father saw no objection to his "Goth" look, and even bought him a pair of those boots .

I lost that battle, of course, and by the time Robin returned to school in the fall of 1984, he had fully assumed the "skinhead" look, complete with a Mohawk haircut that I absolutely hated. If it was only the way he dressed and wore his hair, I'm sure I wouldn't have worried as much as I did, but Robin and his skinhead friends also began to gather in Dupont Circle, which was a gathering spot for the punk-rock scene, and he also began going to a squat house near there. Some of the kids at the house were homeless. Others were privileged children like Robin, and it became clear that drug use was now a big part of his life as well. His grades in school plummeted; his behavior in school was disruptive; his bedroom was always a terrible mess—his whole life was a mess. He was always angry and grew very isolated from his brother, his father, and me.

Peter Sturtevant, the headmaster at Maret told me in conference that he viewed Robin as a boy on a knife edge. He could become a real leader or a true criminal—it was up to him. When Maret officials told Robin he could not return to the school in the autumn of 1986, his father stepped in and registered him at a boarding school run by the Society of Friends north of Philadelphia. But before he began school that fall, I drove Robin up to Princeton to meet with my old friend psychiatrist Peter Mueller, who believed a brain electrical mapping test *might* demonstrate brain deficits that *might* be treatable with medication.

Following testing and evaluation, Mueller was convinced that Robin had a very high IQ, and that the meningitis he had suffered in Maine when he was very young was the root of his attention deficit, hyper-activity and impulsivity, and his occasional migraines. Dr. Mueller prescribed Tegretol, an anticonvulsant that sometimes was prescribed for people who suffered bipolar disorder and attention deficit/hyperactivity disorder. Robin's father was absolutely furious when he learned of the trip and the tests. He said he had not given his consent and maintained that I had taken our son to "the far frontiers of medicine" and had put him in great danger.

The Tegretol worked. Robin complained that it disrupted his sleep, but he also said the medication made him feel as though he had turned on a headlight when he was reading. He could concentrate in ways he couldn't before. Mueller had said Robin likely would need to remain on Tegretol throughout his life, and that was acceptable to me, given the remarkable way in which it helped him. His father, however, furiously disagreed.

I drove him north to the George School in Newtown, Pennsylvania, where I met with the headmaster, who guaranteed me that the school nurse would administer the Tegretol to Robin every day. During our meeting, the headmaster also told me how enthusiastic he and others at the school were to have Robin join them, particularly because he scored so highly on IQ tests, and because he seemed a perfect fit for a new Russian curriculum that was planned. Robin had no aptitude for language or music and, it turned out, was not the star Russian student they had expected.

And Robin remained angry. He felt as though he had been sent away—and he had been, of course. He performed poorly, his grades continued to dive, and at the end of another trying year, he was out. I drove to Pennsylvania to pick him up. But on the day he knew I was picking him up for the summer, he was simply nowhere to be found. In his room, I found the Tegretol pills strewn all over the floor and under his bed and it was obvious that school officials had left it up to him to administer the medication himself, which he had chosen not to do. I waited in his room, and when he finally showed up he was totally stoned on what I presumed was marijuana. He slept in the car throughout the entire trip back to Washington.

Robin's next school was Gonzaga, a Jesuit boys-only school that his brother Alexander attended a few blocks north of the capitol building in Washington. It was during Robin's brief tenure there that he became known as "the candy man," someone who could be counted on to supply an array of drugs to anyone with money to buy them. Gonzaga teachers reported that Robin was very bright and had great potential, but he simply refused to apply himself. He was interested in music and drugs and in very little else, it seemed. His anger was constant, and he directed most of it at me. I was working hard in the brokerage business at Julia Walsh & Sons,. Unlike his father, I was the parent who attempted to discipline him and, according to Robin, I was the only reason his life wasn't perfect, a perspective I know he shared this with his friends.

I was diagnosed with stage-four uterine cancer in 1987. I had surgery the day after the Black Monday Crash on October 19. I spent more than three weeks recovering in the Columbia Hospital for Women. The surgeon made some errors and recovery was difficult. I returned home from the hospital on November 1 eager to see the boys and get into my own bed.

Robin met me as I was coming in the door. He aimed a kiss in my direction, then flew off in a big hurry. Alexander told me to sit down because he had something to tell me. The boys had hosted a Halloween party the night before. There were lots of drugs at the party and one of the girls who attended had swallowed rat poison in an attempt to kill herself. Alexander said they had found her outside Robin's bedroom, rushed her to Georgetown Hospital, then spent the night on the floor outside her room waiting to hear if she would live.

It was quite a homecoming. I was recovering from the surgery but still had a suprapubic catheter and bag to contend with, and the news seemed too much. A teenage girl had tried to *commit suicide* in our house and barely survived. It was almost more than I could believe. Alexander still spent little time with his younger brother except on occasions like this one when they hosted a secret and unchaperoned party. Studious, serious Alexander was acting out and he had begun to use drugs as well. Our collective lives appeared to be spiraling out of control.

Still reeling from what I had just learned, I searched Robin's bedroom and found a small jar containing a dark brown sticky substance. I took it to a police station on Utah Avenue. The officer I showed it to said, "whatever it is, you're the person in possession of it." So, I drove down to Georgetown and asked a derelict-looking man I saw sitting in a doorway, and he suggested I take it to the George Washington Hospital where people in the lab likely could tell me what the substance was.

I did what he suggested, but before I received any news I searched Robin's room again and found a roll of *hundreds* of dollars in cash and a big bag filled with marijuana. I called John and asked him to come over and help me confront Robin when he came home. He did as I asked, and he waited with me for Robin for an hour or so. But then he announced he was hungry and left to "go get some soup."

So, it fell to me to confront Robin alone, and I did my best. He agreed to go with me to Georgetown Hospital where, with the support of the chief of psychiatry, he began a drug-counseling program, one that included frequent drug tests and daily Alcoholics Anonymous meetings. When I spoke with Dr. Joseph Ciancaglini, the headmaster at Gonzaga, he assured me that if Robin's doctors recommended residential treatment and he agreed to it, the school would re-admit him at its conclusion and provide every assistance it could.

Robin kept his appointments with the therapist and strictly followed the program. After a few months, the chief called a conference with the psychiatrist and therapist to assess his situation. Robin, his father, and I were told that he was fully addicted in their opinion and needed residential treatment. John considered this recommendation for only a moment before he turned and said, "Robin, I think you can handle this. Why don't we wait until October and if you're not clean you can go to treatment then?"

That was the end of Robin's counseling, treatment, and daily meetings with other addicts, and he was therefore asked to leave Gonzaga. In 1989, he did eventually graduate from the School Without Walls in downtown Washington—a magnet high school that is part of the district's public-school system. The school was a good fit for him, and he motivated himself enough to graduate, but his personal life continued to slide downward. He walked around town barefoot and with a Guatemalan blanket around his shoulders for warmth. He spent lots of time, many nights included, at a house near Sixteenth and Irving streets where other kids in similar circumstances crashed, and his close friends became boys who were in the drug business.

Robin would sleep at home sometimes but having him in the house was every bit as difficult as worrying about him when he was away. Unbeknownst to me at the time, he had discovered a way to get into the attic from the roof and into the market below, where he and his buddies would steal food, beer, and wine from the Scheele brothers who had treated him with care since he was a little boy. Even worse than that, I discovered that he was dealing marijuana, mushrooms, LSD, and other drugs directly from our house. I told him that was the last straw. I said I had done everything I could think of to help him, telling him that it was my responsibility to raise him and his brother and ensure, as best I could, that he became a productive adult. But I wanted him to know that he couldn't put me at risk. I needed to keep my job and I was not willing to take the chance of getting arrested for having drug dealers and dirty money in my house.

I told Robin he would have to leave. I gave him ten minutes to gather clothes and other stuff to take with him. Then I told him it was time to go. I walked him to the front door and took his key from him. In a light rain, he sat down on the front step and began to cry. He asked if he could go back inside to get something he had forgotten, but I said no.

Leaving Home

Back when the boys and I were first on our own many years before, I knew I had to find some way to support us—and fast. But I hadn't worked for years, didn't have any skills, and the prospect of finding work was not a simple one. A friend, Joyce Huber, told me I needed to learn how to type, which I did. She suggested that I network among my friends to see who might need help, so I did that, too.

Before long I had a call from Tom Donaldson, who was a successful partner and stockbroker at Julia Walsh & Sons. He asked me to come to lunch, and I met him at his office. I asked where his assistant Joanne was, and he said that she had left the firm to go into business with her husband. I asked about his wife Shelah, and he said he said she was not coming. Then he said, "This is your job now." I was flabbergasted. He told me to sit down, so I did. The screen on the desk were blinking away with symbols and numbers that meant nothing to me. I didn't even know the multiplication tables! I started to cry, and Tom said, "Stop that! We don't have time for that, we're really busy here! Put your purse in the drawer and turn your chair around and start answering the phone." So, I did.

I didn't know how to answer a business call; I didn't know anything about business at all. Tom was trading options, and the orders were huge; oil was running, and he also was investing clients' money in gold mines all over Africa. It was just wild, and I couldn't believe my luck. Everyone there seemed to know what they were doing, but nothing made any sense to me. All I knew was that there was a very frantic pace to everything that was going on.

Julia Walsh, who owned the firm, was about six feet tall, had white hair and a big presence—the kind of woman who commanded respect, one of the first females to own her own firm and have her own seat on the New York Stock Exchange, the first female president of the Washington, DC Board of Trade. After a few days she came to me, stood over my desk, and said, "Now, dear, this won't do." I was sure she was firing me, but she said. "Now dear, you have to get registered," which meant that she wanted me to take the Series Seven exam to become a registered stockbroker. Everyone in the office called her "Julia," but I said, "Mrs. Walsh, I can't do that. I can't pass that test."

"I didn't ask you any questions, dear," she said, handing me a big stack of books to take home and study. So, every night for about a year, after I got the boys to bed I sat in a big yellow plaid chair and cried, then studied for an hour or two. Finally, I took the exam and passed it. It was the start of a career I could have never imagined for myself but one for which I was deeply grateful. Eventually, my early fear that I knew nothing lessened and I grew more comfortable. I became a pretty good "rainmaker"—someone who brings in new business.

I was making money at last, paying the bills, and I even bought a television set and a few other things that weren't absolutely essential. All the people at Julia Walsh & Sons were great. They were honest, hard-working, and they believed in doing the best they could for every client.

Robin left home when he was seventeen and Alexander was in college at St. Mary's in southern Maryland. I was happy working with Tom. But eventually, he and Shelah moved to Maine, and I had to begin managing clients on my own—some of whom had more money than I felt prepared to manage on my own. So, I set out to connect with some of the best money managers in the country—most of them from New York. They managed accounts on a fee basis, and I was the client contact. I was able to retain enough major clients to create a respectable book of business. And working with these managers suited both my clients and me. I liked my job—many things about it—but like so many single mothers, I was always worried that I knew so little about how to raise happy and well-adjusted children.

Always very different from his younger brother—less effervescent, less of a thrill-seeker, more interested in books and academics—Alexander graduated in 1987 from Gonzaga College High School in Washington, a Jesuit school for boys where he did well, then was off to St. Mary's, a liberal arts college in Maryland with a good reputation, even if it wasn't the kind of Ivy League school his father would have preferred for him.

St. Mary's, just a hundred miles southeast of Washington, was nonetheless far enough away from home that Alexander felt free from family constraints. He was going to school with girls for the first time and, of course, *they* were an exciting new element in his life. He took with him our wonderful dog named Tiger we had been given by our friend Tommy Sims when he contracted AIDS. Tiger and Andrew became a pair. Andrew developed writing skills, wrote poetry, and enjoyed school, but St. Mary's was also the place where his life took a dark turn.

He had begun drinking in high school, but at St. Mary's he began to drink heavily. He started experimenting with drugs, too. He paid lip service to wanting to learn the guitar, but mostly he just wanted to be high. To his credit, he eventually cut back on his drinking, but he increasingly used marijuana, cocaine, crack, and even heroin—whatever came his way. He was young and, like so many his age, he thought he was indestructible. He continued to be a good student and was accepted to St. Michael's College at Oxford University, where he studied literature and enjoyed the Oxford life.

He telephoned me from England on his twenty-first birthday in August, not long after he arrived. He sounded a bit apprehensive but also worldly and optimistic, and I remember telling him that his brother Robin had recently called from rural northern California, where he was making ends meet by working in the illegal but nonetheless locally sanctioned marijuana business. Alexander wanted me to send flannel shirts and jeans from The Gap to ward off the incessantly damp English weather. I told him I was worried about Robin, but Alexander seemed uninterested in his brother, so I let the subject drop.

Robin had gone from wearing a mohawk and living the punk life in Washington to dreadlocks and pot in outpost California in only three years. And it was a journey that was punctuated by music. Back when punk first began to catch his attention, Washington had become a center of the American punk-rock scene. Bands like State of Alert, Black Flag, and the Rollins Band, all featuring Washingtonian Henry Rollins, and Minor Threat and Fugazi, led by another Washingtonian, Ian MacKaye, played constantly at clubs and warehouses in the Dupont Circle area. They pioneered a kind of angry, nihilistic music that had enormous appeal for kids like him.

He later got into reggae, largely because of the influence of local Jamaican kids he emulated. Now, he wanted to wear dreadlocks like the Jamaicans did, and when "the hippie bus drove by," as he put it, he jumped on. The seductive lure of the community created by the kids who followed The Grateful Dead became a very powerful attraction for him. He and fifty or so of his closest friends began traveling to the Dead's infamous jam-band concerts throughout the United States, traveling in Volkswagen microbuses or anything that rolled and had a motor. At many dozens of live events each year, they would set up "Shakedown Street"—so dubbed after a Grateful Dead song—in the parking lots of the arenas and festival sites where the Dead played. Shakedown Street was a very loosely controlled vending area where hundreds of "Deadheads" could sell vegetarian food, clothing, jewelry, and alcohol to other attendees. Their income supported their travel to the next concert on the schedule, and Robin's niche was selling illicit drugs. Known as "The Candy Man" in Washington, Robin became one of the traveling Deadheads whose Shakedown Street wares featured marijuana, peyote, psychedelic mushrooms, the purple microdot form of LSD, and even rarer hallucinogens like ayahuasca and ibogaine. Robin's good friend Chris Kelly, who had grown up in nearby Baltimore and who first connected with him in the Washington punk scene, had jumped on the hippie bus early on, and Chris actually worked for the band and made good money. Robin's candy-man vending didn't make him much, on the other hand, but he had access to everything, and he sold everything. And it provided enough income to keep him on the road.

The life of a Deadhead also provided him a sense of brotherhood he otherwise did not have, a sense of tribal belonging, and the belief that he and the Deadheads he traveled with were creating a brave new world where peace and love would one day rule the world. It was a life that was enormously appealing to Robin, and it was where he met and fell in love with Nancy Sinkler.

I remember Robin calling at some point during his first years on the road to tell me that he had met someone very special, and that he wanted to bring her home to meet me. He told me he was sure I would like her,. When they arrived, I insisted that they leave all their clothes and gear outside and shower before we sat down together in the living room. I was afraid that they had lice or bedbugs or something worse, and they cheerfully acquiesced. And Robin was right. I liked Nancy very much. In fact, I thought she was perfect.

Nancy had grown up in Rhode Island on a farm where her parents raised racehorses. She had a gentle, beatific quality about her, a calmness in counterpoint to Robin's more manic nature. She was a charming hippie-girl who had been tested by fire—literally. On a trip to India with a boy she knew, she had been badly burned when a thin cotton skirt she was wearing caught fire. Her father flew to be near her and to do what he could to help her because she was in a remote area and there was no hospital nearby. For hours every day for weeks, Nancy's father would drip water from a block of ice onto the burns on her back and legs. She survived and her father ultimately chartered a plane to bring her home. The pain eventually subsided. Her scars were fading, and once she was well Nancy chose to follow the Grateful Dead, just as Robin had.

I was happy for Robin to have found such a girl, someone so suited to him and his own particular challenges. I imagined that she would turn his life around. I know Robin was pleased that I liked her, and as they left to continue their travels with the Grateful Dead, I imagined that with a girl like Nancy in his life Robin and I would become close again, just as we were back when he was a little boy.

When Alexander's year at Oxford was over, he returned to St. Mary's, where he met the lovely, dark-haired Anne Corter, and they fell in love. When he and Anne graduated, he got a summer job working with Washington's legendary housing and redevelopment advocate Marilyn Melkonian, and he planned to begin a master's program in literature at Catholic University in Washington in the fall. Anne also got a job in the city, and I was delighted to have the two of them come to live on the third floor in the apartment over Scheele's. Tiger came, too, and he was happy as well. They were young and in love, and soon they got engaged and moved to a charming garden apartment on Twenty-Second Street.

As time went on, I noticed how thin Anne was becoming and that even in the summer heat she constantly wore long-sleeved shirts. In retrospect, I must have been blind not to realize how dramatically drugs had become part of their lives—heavy drugs, the kind that ruin lives. Alexander had proven his ability to drink heavily and use all kinds of illegal substances yet still get good grades while he was at St. Mary's. Now he was apparently coping in much the same way in his job. But he and Anne, I now know, made a pact to get straight not long after they got their own apartment—at least straight after a fashion. At a party, they announced to friends that they were cleaning things up. No more shooting heroin, they told everyone in attendance, most of whom were junkies themselves. No more smoking crack. And living a more responsible life was going to save them tons of money and improve their health. Life was going to be great.

But one day I got a call from Alexander, clearly in distress, asking me to please come pick them up at Rose Park. His hand was swollen as big as a baseball mitt when I arrived. He was wildly agitated, and Anne looked like she couldn't have weighed more than a hundred pounds, and both were clearly very sick. With great difficulty, I got them into the car and drove them to George Washington Hospital and checked them into the emergency room.

I was ill with pneumonia and was on a medication that required me to eat every couple of hours. I went to the hospital cafeteria to get a sandwich or something and when I came back to the emergency room, it was crawling with police. I asked what was going on and was told that a young man had tried to break into the locked medicine cabinet. I instantly knew who that young man was.

The police wanted to haul both Alexander and Anne off to another hospital. My own physician, Joel Guiterman intervened and arranged for them to be admitted to Suburban Hospital in Bethesda, which had a program for drug addicts. I called Anne's mother, and she joined me and Alexander and Anne—who by now was so sick she couldn't walk—and I drove the four of us to Suburban, even though I was ill myself.

Soon after our arrival, they sent Alexander up to a room for evaluation and I went with him, leaving Anne with her mother. He was quiet, and seemed okay, but the moment we were alone he picked up a chest of drawers and tried to throw it at me, screaming that he hated me and that I was the reason he and Anne were in such trouble. Within seconds, he calmed down and was sorry for the violence. He began to weep, begged me to take care of Tiger, and asked where Anne was. When he blew up a second time only a couple of minutes later, I told him I couldn't take it and I left.

Just before I left the hospital, I called a cousin, John Fleming in Philadelphia, who had years of experience in Alcoholic Anonymous, to see if he could help get Anne and Alexander into Hazelton, the well-known treatment center in Minnesota. John said he thought he could help. I spoke with Anne's mother to tell her what was underway, then I went home to take care of myself.

It was getting dark, but I realized that Tiger was alone at Alexander and Anne's apartment. I drove there, but the sliding-glass door was broken an unkempt man I presumed was a druggie or dealer was sitting inside. I called out, telling him to leave, or I would kill him. He left in a hurry. The door was off its hinges, and when I went inside, I saw a fold-out couch in the living room covered with blood. I took off my shoes and went the spiral stairs just to see what was what—but then I realized that it wasn't safe for me to be there. When I came downstairs, my shoes were gone, so I took Tiger in a hurray and went home.

Back at the apartment, I called my best friend Betsy Glaeser, who at that time ran the capital markets for Mobile Oil, and my dear friend Bud Veech, a chief scientist at the National Institutes of Health, and told each of them a bit about what had happened that afternoon. They rushed over. Bud arrived with a huge bundle of flowers in his arms, and he reminded me that I really needed to call John, Alexander's father. So, I did, and, all-too-predicably, he exploded in a verbal rage—lots of noise but no help.

When I explained that my cousin John Fleming had been told that Hazelton had a space for Anne but no opening for a male, Bud got on the phone and reached Hazelton's director, telling him that if he would agree to take Alexander, he would fly out there and lecture free of charge. The pitch worked. Alexander would be admitted to Hazelton, but he had to get there first, and I was too sick to travel.

But was an unusual guy—and a wonderful friend who was *very* smart. He had been first in his class at Harvard Medical School, and first at Oxford. Many years before that night helping us, he had been one of ten survivors of a plane crash in New Hampshire. Although his back was broken, he had pulled the other survivors out of the plane and rolled them down a hill and away from the burning plane. He spent five months strapped into a Striker frame in a hospital. His spine continued to be at risk from another potential injury, and

I was surprised when he volunteered to fly with Alexander to Minnesota, get him admitted to Hazelton, then return the same day.

If Alexander attacked Bud the way he had attacked me at Suburban Hospital, his spine could be severed, and he could be paralyzed. I was bowled over by his bravery and the kindness of his offer. I told him how grateful I was.

Betsy was calm and clear-headed and arranged all the travel plans. The two of them fixed dinner for the three of us, and Bud explained that he had called Suburban and Alexander would be sedated and ready to travel later that night. Betsy had secured two seats on a direct flight. She told me to pick Bud up at his house at two in the morning. He would get a few hours' sleep, then together he and I would go to Suburban, pick up Alexander and go to National airport, where they would board their flight.

As soon as Bud was gone, Betsy looked at me and said, "Let's go." We went to Alexander's apartment to look for some family jewelry that included a diamond ring I had given to Alexander to give to Anne. I was very worried about Betsy going into that place alone—where anyone could enter, and anything could happen.

Betsy was a clever searcher, and she found Anne's jewelry bag—hidden in the pocket of one of Alexander's suits, which was inside a dry-cleaner's bag. With it in hand, we left as quickly as we could. Betsy promised me that she would scrub herself from head to toe with antibacterial soap before she went to bed. There was no telling what bugs we might have picked up, even in the few minutes we were there. Blood was everywhere, and I couldn't help but imagine every manner of contagion from dirty needles or whatever.

When Bud and I picked Alexander up at Suburban Hospital, he was heavily sedated, as promised, and I brought Tiger along to help keep him calm. We parked and I went to the waiting area, which was empty at that hour, with Bud and Alexander and sat with them. All of a sudden, Alexander announced that we were trying to trick him into going to Hazelton by telling him that Anne was there. Bud got on the phone to Hazelton in the middle of the night and explained the situation. The staff person there miraculously located Anne and she spoke with Alexander by phone, assuring him that she was there and that she wanted him to come as soon as possible.

The concourse at National Airport was all but deserted that time of night and we had to wait long enough that at some point I decided to walk over to a magazine kiosk to look for something to read. Just as I did, Alexander sprang to his feet and ran toward me, saying he was going to kill me and trying to hit me with the bag he was carrying. Two cops came rushing to my aid and got hold of Alexander and told me they were going to take him to a police car outside and take him away. I asked them if I could speak to the head of security before they did anything.

When he arrived, I explained that Alexander was on his way to Hazelton, a drug treatment center, and that it was truly his last hope. The man escorting him, I said, was a physician and this was my suggestion: let Alexander and the doctor board the plane first, then Bud would give him enough sedative to "knock an elephant out for a month." Once that was done, the other passengers could board, and if there was a problem of any kind, Alexander could be pulled off the plane quickly and taken into custody. Luckily, the security official agreed.

Alexander and Bud boarded, and I waited, and each minute that passed seemed like an hour. It was the worst moment of my life. All I could do was pray that Alexander would stay sedated, and the plane would take off. There was still every chance that something could go terribly wrong. I knew it would have been hard for Alexander to seriously hurt me. But given Bud's damaged spine, it was entirely possible that Andrew could kill him if he went into another rage.

I waited. It seemed to take forever for the plane to leave the gate, but at last it did. I stood by a bank of windows, watching and waiting until finally the plane lifted into the sky. I thanked Bud and God.

The recovery journey for Alexander and Anne was only just beginning, and they would have to negotiate many hurdles along the way, but, little by little, I began to be sure that they were in the right place. *Both* my sons were addicts, and they had come to their addictions separately and in very different ways. It was impossible for me not to question from that time forward whether *I* was responsible. Did my contentious divorce and awful relationship with their father cause the boys to falter? Did the fact that they were raised in privilege but also without any money play a part? Was it my mothering style? Was it me? *Both* my sons were addicts, and it was impossible for me not to presume that somehow I was the reason why.

Alexander was now in treatment, and he was in love. Robin, too, had a wonderful young woman in his life. Although he continued to follow the Grateful Dead with Nancy he would call from time to time, and Robin or the two of them would visit for a couple of days once or twice a year. Both boys were now young men, and both could still be sweet. Following a short visit at Christmas in 1989—and Christmas above Scheele's Market had always been special—I found this note that Robin had written for me:

> Dear Mom, Our life together thus far has been a turbulent ride. Sometimes we seemed so close and other times so far. I never forgot, though, how much you love me, and I hope you always knew that my love was with you also. I understand that sometimes this love is hard to see, but please remember that it was always there. . . . I feel that I am dancing in the light and I want to share it with you but you feel that I am drowning in the hole and want desperately to save me. . . . I also want to say that this Christmas has been a special one for me because I have been away for so long. Having forgotten what home was like, it was nice to learn what a warm and friendly place it is to be. I love you, Robin

He drew a peace symbol after his name.

The Accident

Robin seldom let me know much in advance, but his visits home continued. I'm sure his desire was at least as much to stay in touch with the "homies" he still cared about as it was to see either his father or me. But at least when Robin and I were infrequently together, the sight of him offered visual proof that he was alive and okay, if not living the life I had hoped for him. But this time, his return home was the catalyst for a horrifying accident that would profoundly affect him for all the years ahead.

Just before 11:00 o'clock on a Tuesday night in the first days of July 1991, Robin and a friend entered the Woodley-Park Zoo station of the Washington Metro. They boarded a train and traveled the single stop to the Dupont Circle station, where they got off the train and rode an escalator from the underground station up to its 19th Street exit, en route to see the new film *Terminator 2: Judgement Day*. As Robin was about to step off the escalator, the toe of his right sneaker was suddenly trapped between the metal step and the "comb plate" at the top of the escalator.

Robin desperately tried to pull his foot free, but the moving escalator drew it still farther under the comb plate and as his foot went in he was thrown onto his back. Robin screamed for someone to turn off the escalator, but it continued to pull his foot farther under the comb plate and grind his right foot. Robin's friend jumped onto the other side of the escalator and frantically ran to a control booth, but an operator there told him he could not turn off the escalator until the police arrived.

No one could locate an emergency stop button, so the escalator continued to grind his foot for fully ten minutes before at last a homeless man located the emergency button at the top of the escalator and stopped it.

Members of the Metropolitan Fire Department arrived on the scene and, with the help of a "jaws of life" hydraulic tool, were able to widen the gap between the escalator's comb plate and treads. As rescue workers attempted to lift the comb plate enough to remove Robin's foot, the plate slipped and smashed his already mangled foot, but the second attempt was successful. An ambulance took him to the Georgetown University Hospital emergency room, where he would undergo multiple surgeries in hopes of saving his foot.

I received a telephone call with news of the accident when Robin was in the emergency room, and when I arrived a few minutes later, I found him lying in a cubicle with drawn curtains. Lots of medical personnel were there, but no one had yet given him anything for pain. Robin was conscious, but barely. From what I could observe, nothing remained of his right foot except the sole, a few toes and what appeared to be pulsing red hamburger. He kept asking, "Why did this happen to me? I tried to be a good person."

When I asked one of the doctors what would happen next, I was told that they would simply "clean it up," meaning amputate his foot. Although I had been hugely distraught up to that moment, I suddenly felt cold and calm, and I said no. I asked the doctors to find a surgeon with experience treating battlefield injuries. They did. Dr. Christopher Attinger, a plastic surgeon who had served in Vietnam and had an extensive and distinguished record, came in and took charge.

The first surgeries were designed to debride Robin's foot, cleaning it and removing dirt and debris. Dr. Attinger removed a nine-inch by twelve-inch piece of skin with its blood supply from Robin's back and grafted it, making a cover of the top of the foot. Then he stretched the skin that remained on his back and fastened it together with huge metal staples. The constant pain was beyond description, and between each surgery his days were also filled with panic and relentless vomiting. Several times, he went into shock, turned gray and looked close to death, before his blood was transfused. Dr. Attinger explained that people often die not from the wound itself but from shock—which was far more likely to kill him than the foot injury was.

Robin's girlfriend Nancy flew to Washington from California as soon as she could, and Robin was hugely relieved to see her. She had a kind of inner peace and calmness about her that gave Robin—and me—solace and comfort. She spent her first four nights in town at the hospital with Robin rather than with me, and I was grateful to her for being there for him.

Robin was given morphine via injection every hour or so. The objective, we were told, was simply to keep the pain under at least some control, but the pain was horrendous. It induced chills, nausea, depression, and raw fear. None of us had any certainty that he would survive. Medical personnel had placed drains in his injured foot and back, inserted urinary and epidural catheters, and put him on oxygen. The days crawled by at a merciless pace, and he continued to ask, "What did I do to deserve this?" And he often wondered aloud whether he would ever walk again.

I was contacted by a South African photographer named Constance Larrabee who had been married to my father's best friend, who wanted me to know about a world-famous surgeon whose specialty was foot and ankle injuries. When I spoke with him by phone, he was intrigued by the case and spoke with Dr. Attinger. The two surgeons agreed to collaborate and attempt to save Robin's foot.

Prior to a final, ten-hour surgery In Baltimore, Dr. Myerson explained to Robin, Nancy, and me that there was "extensive, ruinous damage to bones and joints and the foot extensors are gone." He said he had hoped that he could make one tendon serve both sides of the foot, but now that was clearly not possible. He told Robin he *would* walk again, but he would likely walk with a limp.

The day before the surgery, Robin was extremely upset and anxious when I arrived to visit him. He told me his father had sent two lawyers to talk with him and they had been demanding and aggressive. A few days following the surgery, two more personal-injury lawyers arrived wearing bright white shirts and expensive suits and each had a contract in his pocket ready for signing. They treated Robin and me dismissively, and it was clear that they were already counting the money they would make from what appeared to be a slam-dunk case. They seemed oblivious to Robin's condition or state of mind.

Robin declined to sign, and the lawyers left. It wasn't until a few days later—when Robin had begun to be more lucid and was more comfortable than he had been from the beginning—that another lawyer, Brendan Sullivan, walked in late one afternoon. He wore a plain gray suit; his hair was as gray as his suit. He acknowledged Nancy and me and quickly sat down near Robin's bed and said in a very quiet voice how sorry he was about the accident and how he hoped nothing like it would ever happen to anyone again. He added that he would help Robin legally if that was what he wanted or would help him find a lawyer of whom he approved..

There was something caring and real about Brendan, and we all soon fell under his quiet spell. Robin said he wanted Brendan to take the case, and it was the first time since the accident that we felt relieved.

Recovery came slowly. But eventually Robin could sit in a chair for a short while. A few days later, we wheeled him out to the hospital patio for a bit of sunshine. He was terribly frightened of each new experience, but he endured them, and on July 18 he was released from Georgetown and came home to the apartment. Jack and his wife Sally, whom I liked and could easily talk to, came to visit and Sally brought soups and food she knew Robin liked. A physical therapist came several times to work on Robin's shoulder, which had become immobilized during the surgery to take the skin from his back, and Brendan often came to observe the therapy and talk.

When Brendan wanted to discuss Robin's case with me at his firm, he picked me up in his car and took me to the main conference room at Williams & Connolly, where he was a senior partner. With us was one of his colleagues, Allan Galbraith, whom I knew after a fashion. Brendan wanted to hear about Robin's early childhood and life before the accident. He also wanted to know if he had been in possession of any drugs on the day of the accident.

I told Brendan that I didn't want to discuss Robin's early years in front of Galbraith. He explained that Galbraith was his co-counsel and assured me that nothing I told them would ever leave the room. I explained that it was Galbraith's wife Sarah who had polled the children's mothers back when Robin was a student at Beauvoir, then had told me she had canvassed the mothers and that none of the kids would attend his birthday party. I didn't believe for one minute that Galbraith could resist sharing juicy stories about Robin's past with his wife. Brendan understood that and took Galbraith off the case.

Brendan cautioned all of us that a case like this might take years before it would go to court. And he showed us the draft of a seven-count complaint Williams & Conolly planned to bring against the Metro Authority, Schindler Elevator Company, which inspected and maintained the escalator, and Westinghouse Electric Corporation, manufacturer of the escalator that had virtually destroyed Robin's foot. As drafted, the suit requested $70 million in compensatory damages and $10 million in punitive damages from the three defendants. Brendan privately estimated that, in the end, a jury ruling of $10 million to $15 million was likely, but he also cautioned that you couldn't count on receiving a penny until a case was adjudicated in court.

He instructed Robin to return to California when he was strong enough, to go to school or get a job, and to stay out of trouble. Because of Dr. Myerson's extraordinary skill and dedication, Robin was able to keep his right foot—or semblance of a foot—and he went back to northern California and resumed his life with Nancy. But clearly, Robin now presumed that an enormous financial windfall would be coming his way, and he did not enroll in college or get a job.

I was concerned and wrote to him, saying, in part, "An accident is a random event. There are so many things in life over which we have no control. . . . What if there is a settlement large enough to do more than cover medical and legal bills and give you financial protection in case you need future medical care? . . . Maybe, in this time before a settlement or trial it's possible to consider how to move the course of your life in a new direction." I just wanted to share my thoughts, and to tell him how much I loved him.

In March 1992, we learned that in discovery Sullivan and his colleagues had been informed that on the day of the accident eight months before, Metro police searching for evidence had found a small amount of hashish in his pocket. Robin had sworn to Brendan that he was *not* carrying any drugs at the time of the accident. Sullivan and his firm had devoted enormous resources to the case, but lying was unacceptable, and he said he could not represent Robin if he could not trust his confidential statements. Clearly, he could not. It was as simple as that.

Sullivan and Williams & Conolly formally dropped the case, and Robin's father stepped in and brought Robert Cave on board, a lawyer at Hogan & Hartson who had met with us while Peter was still in the hospital. John liked Cave a lot, but I did not. I had been present when Cave met with Robin, and not once did Cave speak directly to him. He aimed all his comments to Robin's father, and three times I heard him say that "this case will be *fun*!"

Robin had new representation now. The case would drag on and the "fun" would continue for six more years.

California

Before Robin's terrible accident at the Dupont Circle Metro station, he and Nancy had decided they would no longer follow the Grateful Dead from concert to concert. When Robin told friends he was moving to Trinidad, many presumed he meant the island in the Caribbean—because he still wore his blond hair in dreadlocks and remained a fan of reggae music—but, in fact, he wanted to move to the town of Trinidad in Humboldt County in far northern California. He planned to give up selling drugs to consumers in favor of the opportunity to make *real* money growing marijuana.

Humboldt County, up on the Oregon border, is a remote place of towering redwood trees, clear rivers and streams, and a forbidding but beautifully rocky coastline. In the 1970s, young hippies and back-to-the-landers discovered that marijuana grew remarkably well in the Humboldt region's rich soil. Its hot days, cool nights, and high humidity were important, too, and there was good money to be made in growing and selling pot.

By the time Robin arrived in 1990, about eighty percent of all the marijuana consumed in the United States was grown in Humboldt and neighboring Mendocino and Trinity counties—and that was a *lot* of marijuana. The United States government had declared war on Mexican marijuana, where most of the U.S. supply had previously come from. As the supply from Mexico waned and consumer worries about herbicide-tainted Mexican marijuana grew, farmers in Humboldt saw the opportunity to fill the void by producing organic marijuana that was carefully—and secretly—grown in the shadow of the redwoods. Growers in the Humboldt region began to focus on cultivating female plants, which produced the flowers that created the highs, and these hippies-turned-self-taught-botanists began breeding more and more potent marijuana strains.

It was a world that looked like heaven when Robin first visited. It quicky became the place he wanted to make his home. Both he and Nancy were very happy in the beginning. They rented a dingy apartment in Arcata, a town just a few miles from Trinidad, and before too long, Robin was making money selling the pot he grew—at a time when local law enforcement gave the illegal growing very little attention.

Like most of his fellow farmers, the growing operations Robin eventually constructed were off-grid and self-sustainable. Across the three-county area, young growers located their operations in barns and sheds and abandoned warehouses. Robin built a huge undergrown greenhouse—known casually as "the bunker"—that he supplied with electricity from generators and water from wells and complex diversions from creeks. Like everyone else in his line of work, he did business with handshakes, verbal agreements, and cash—mountains of cash. Robin's old friend Chris Kelly remembers visiting one time and helping Robin bury a million dollars in cash in a white plastic picnic cooler. He also remembers Robin calling him months later to see if Chris remembered where they had buried the cooler because he himself could not.

It was an idyllic life for a kid like him. Robin had always loved nature and the outdoors, loved the water, and during his Grateful Dead years he had become a vegan and said the only creed he believed in was one centered on peace and love. In Humboldt, he made a lot of money. He worked hard and the difficulty concentrating he had had since his school days didn't get in his way. He surfed as often as he wanted, and he took an impish kind of delight in telling people that the big scar on his back and his damaged foot were the result of a shark attack. "Shark Attack" became his nickname, in fact, and he became something of a local legend.

As he explains it, the enormous value of the crop he grew necessitated protecting it with weapons. he began stockpiling a huge arsenal—rifles, pistols, assault weapons, mortars, mines, even rocket launchers—and he discovered that there was something about firearms he really liked. Guns were exciting, dangerous, risky. Their presence brought a kind of adrenaline rush to the most mundane activities and obligations. Robin had always been a thrill seeker and weapons were exhilarating to him.

As more and more gangsters from southern California began to move up to Humboldt, drawn by both the pot, the criminality, and the big money that came with it, Robin connected with a group of young men from San Diego who thought he was something special. He began to travel south to San Diego regularly, and there he and a local tough guy named Armando Flores became close friends—surfing all day and spending money lavishly in clubs at night. And they spent time planning ways to make even more money by importing cocaine, marijuana, and other drugs across the nearby Mexican border. They also made silencers for pistols and exported them to northern Mexico where the silencers were in high demand by narco-traffickers to whom he was well-connected.

It was heady, exciting, and more than a little dangerous, and Robin loved it. He began shipping significant quantities of pot, cocaine, and LSD back to criminal contacts he maintained in the Washington and Baltimore areas, and he was in thrall with what he thought was a glamorous underground life. Then, on September 17, 1992, Robin and two other men were arrested at a Days Inn in San Diego and charged with possession and intent to sell 128 pounds of marijuana.

Armando escaped arrest; Robin was bailed out of jail by his father. He and the two others who were arrested with him pleaded guilty and Robin was freed until his sentencing date on January 12, 1993. My cousin Jack Polk, whose daughter had been arrested when drugs were found on a friend's boat in the Caribbean, strongly encouraged me to attend. He was convinced that if the judge saw that I was a reputable mother in strong support of her son, it might make a difference. So, I flew to San Diego and attended the trial, wearing a classic black suit, a crisp white shirt, and pearls. I looked as much like a woman in finance as it was possible to look.

Robin had cut off his dreadlocks, and I made sure he appeared in court in a clean, V-neck sweater I had bought for him, which he wore over a white Oxford shirt. And my cousin was right—it did make a difference. The judge said from the bench that he could see that Robin had the support of his family and because of that the court was giving him the lightest sentence of the group—eighty days followed by three years' probation. There was nothing I could do, nothing but watch as the deputies handcuffed my boy and took him to jail.

My good friend Janice Frey was with me in San Diego, and back the hotel after court I was unnerved and couldn't calm down. I told her I felt like a Mexican jumping bean. I couldn't sit still, and I couldn't bear the idea of going to a restaurant or staying couped up in a hotel room. Janice was a walker, so she suggested we take a walk. I could have walked to Arkansas that afternoon. We walked for hours as I tried to cope with the fact that my son was going to jail. It was getting dark; Janice was getting cold, and I offered her my coat. Finally, we hailed a taxi and returned to our hotel, but I was still in shock. Watching your child get convicted and sentenced as a criminal, then seeing taken down the rabbit hole to jail is an experience I would never wish on anyone. It was awful. But the experience was horrible for Robin as well as me. He was constantly cold and afraid that he would be knifed—or worse.

Robin was twenty-one years old and had a terribly mangled foot that remained in some danger of being amputated. His conviction of a felony in California left the outcome of his civil case in Washington very much in doubt. Robert Grimes, his defense lawyer in San Diego, wrote to Robert Cave, the lead personal injury lawyer in Washington, offering to do what he could to get Robin's conviction reduced to a misdemeanor, but he warned that succeeding quickly was unlikely. "I believe that it is more likely than not that a judge would reduce the conviction to a misdemeanor after a reasonable period of time on probation," he wrote. But he cautioned that, in his experience, a judge would be unlikely to expunge the conviction until the full three years of probation were concluded, and provided that Robin conducted himself as a very upstanding young man during that time.

Robin had already made his potential success in civil court far more complicated by having hashish in his possession on the night of the accident and lying to his first lawyer about it. And now that he had been convicted of possession of marijuana for sale—a felony—who knew how his civil case would go? The civil case against the Metro and the escalator makers couldn't be delayed indefinitely. He wrote to me from jail in San Diego:

Dear Mom, Tonight is my last night in jail and I've finally sat down to write you. Sorry it took so long. Needless to say I'll be glad when this experience is over but it certainly has been an eye opener. . . . I expect life will be different now, not just without money and pot but also with all the probation restrictions and school or work. I guess I'm a little worried that it will be boring knowing full well that I'm someone who craves excitement . . .

He added that he would see me in Washington soon, and said he wanted to meet with doctors to see if additional operations might help his foot as well as meet with the lawyers whom he still believed would win a multi-million dollar settlement and make him rich.

Robin swore that smoking—and selling—pot were his only illegal activities. But he was lying again. Sometime later he showed me a poem he had written while he was in jail. It was long and rambling and heroin focused.

Stone walls do not a prison make
Nor iron bars a cage
But heroin has locked me up tight
And turned me to a slave....
I know what happened, I tried the needle,
Now it's on.
So, on and on this rail I ride,
Robbing, cheating, dealing,
That's what I do to survive.
It's heroin, my friend, or the devil himself.
It's taken my friends and family and hope.
But do I care? No, I don't,
Just want that shot of hardcore dope....
Now I'm kicking hard on the jailhouse floor.
Fightin' with boys as I came through the door.
You buy it, you try it
The first time's fun.
Then before you know it
The battle is on....
Now I'm in jail kickin' cold turkey,
Got to squab some guy for trying to punk me.
Now my ass is beat and I'm all dope sick,
What I wouldn't give for just one hit.

Robin was released from jail on March 25, 1993, and he returned to the apartment he shared with Nancy in Arcata. At first, he attempted to be the model citizen his terms of parole required him to be, but the lure of the very big money in the marijuana trade in northern California proved to be too much for him to resist and he got back into the growing business before long.

On March 30, 1994, Nancy gave birth to a boy she and Robin named Matthew. Soon after the baby was born, Nancy's mother, whose name was also Nancy, and I flew out to Eureka—the town a few miles southwest of Arcata where they were living. We shared a room at a Holiday Inn and were excited to go meet our new grandson. But we were shocked by the condition of their apartment. A dirty mattress lay on the floor; the bedside table was an upside-down orange crate; there was no sort of nursery or even a bassinette for the baby, and the kitchen and bathroom were filthy. Young Nancy was as sweet and loving as ever, but Robin was high on marijuana virtually the whole time we were there.

Grandma Nancy and I couldn't imagine our beautiful little grandson living in this mess, so we went shopping and bought a new bed, shower curtain, some outdoor furniture, flowers, and lots of cleaning supplies. Then we went back to the apartment and started scrubbing. At the end of the day, the five of us went to a Eureka restaurant. Nancy was happy with her new son, of course, and we did our best to make it a nice evening despite the fact that Robin was extremely rude to all of us throughout the meal.

A few weeks after our trip, I received a note from Nancy's mother, telling me that she and her husband Dick continued to believe in Nancy and Robin as a couple, but she added, "I hope things continue to work out for them and that Robin becomes more and more committed to their 'family.' I have only one real regret. I actually heard Nancy say that Robin was waiting around for his expected settlement, and I truly hate to see anyone living their life that way, expecting the pie in the sky to fall in his lap."

She was right, of course. Robin was counting on a huge settlement from the Washington Metro, and we all hoped something more could be done medically for his foot. Dr. Mark Myerson, who practiced in nearby Baltimore, believed he could add one more piece to the foot reconstruction he had earlier performed with Dr. Attinger. Dr. Myerson did a long and complex fourth surgery in which he redirected an artery in Robin's right foot, giving it a much better blood supply than it otherwise would have had. He had survived the accident. He could walk and before long he could resume his life in almost every way, Dr. Attinger assured him.

Robin returned to Washington, this time accompanied by Nancy, for the start of his trial on Monday, April 7, 1997. The following day, the *Washington*

Post reported, "Richards [testified that] he remembers feeling the machine cut into his flesh and bones and the incredible pressure on his foot as it disappeared under the flat metal platform." When his foot was finally freed many minutes later, his foot "looked like a skeleton in biology class, Richards said."

The defense attorneys representing Metro focused on what they said was Robin's own negligence. He was likely under the influence of drugs at the time of the accident, they contended, because a small amount of hashish had been found in this possession. It was the kind of evidence that the mostly black jury appeared very influenced by. Virtually every juror had ridden the Metro hundreds of times without incident; most had probably traveled to the courthouse on the Metro that morning, in fact. They said in court that in their eyes, Robin was a spoiled, rich, white kid from Georgetown who didn't *deserve* his injury but who likely contributed to it.

Prior to Nancy's testimony, I helped her dress for court. She wore a cream-colored collarless blouse and a simple gathered blueprint skirt. Her dress and quiet manner made her seem sweet and innocent, and her testimony focused on the pain Robin had suffered and the fact that his foot continued to smell—something some jurors appeared to note with horror.

Robert Cave did an excellent job making the case against Metro, despite the challenge of Robin possessing hashish. He had asked Robin's family to stay out of the courtroom during the several days of testimony, but John nonetheless did otherwise, sitting prominently in the courtroom each day and constantly scribbling on a yellow legal pad during the proceedings—something that likely didn't help his son's cause.

A week after the trial had begun, the jury returned a verdict after only three hours of deliberations. The jurors found "that Richards's foot was caught in the top of the escalator because Meto failed to keep it properly maintained . . . and his right foot was pulled in up to his ankle under what amounted to about 4,000 pounds of pressure," according to the *Post*. But instead of the $15 million or so Robin had been counting on in damages, the jury's award was $800,000, despite the fact that "his foot is bloated and distorted and most of his toes are 'dead.'"

Robin left the courtroom in tears, in part, I suspect, because he had borrowed heavily against the much larger amount he was expecting to receive. Cave told the *Post* that "Money can't compensate for this," as he left the courthouse. I refrained from asking him about his comment six years before that the case would be "fun" because I knew that, for all of us, it most certainly had *not* been a good time.

"The Portal of Evil"

They were both young adults now—Alexander and Robin. Neither lived at home any longer; they were not particularly close, and never had been. Yet separately, in different ways and perhaps for different reasons, both had become addicts. It was crushing to me to consider this fact. Both their father John and I were drinkers, but we were not drunks. I don't believe either of us had *ever* blacked out from drinking. Was the divorce and the ill will that continued to fester between their father and me the reason for their addictions? Were both my sons addicts because they had grown up with too little money or, ironically, too great a sense of privilege? Had I been too consumed with my career, friendships, and relationships to be there for my sons when they needed me?

The answer to that last question was no, I wanted to believe. The boys had always been *far* more important to me than anything else. I had to be the disciplinarian in the family while their father simply played the role of occasional pal. Was that the cause? Surely there was a reason why each of my sons had chosen a very self-destructive path just as his life was truly getting underway. I was desperate for an explanation, a plausible answer to the question *why*. But answers proved to be cruelly elusive. And at least I was wise enough to know that I could not *demand* drug-free lives of my sons. Their lives were theirs to live. All I could do was offer unwavering love and support. But often that seemed like very little.

At Hazelton, Anne and Alexander were allowed to walk together for a brief time each afternoon. I was surprised, but that decision helped me recognize how much their caregivers were paying attention to them as individuals. They saw, as I did, how in love the two young people were, and they assessed that a bit of time together each day was therapeutic. Anne and I had become close over time and we remained close, but Anne didn't call me regularly during her twenty-eight-day inpatient rehab at Hazelton.

Alexander, however, telephoned constantly. Sometimes he was worried about how Tiger was doing, and he was often sweet and tender, expressing sorrow about how he had treated me and others. Other times, he continued to be furious at me, lashing out, calling me names, and telling me I was the cause of all his problems. Sometimes, he was alternatively apologetic and angry during the few minutes of a single phone call.

At the end of a month of commitment, Anne made the decision to go to New Jersey with a man who had completed inpatient rehab as well. He was a British "remittance man" who received a large monthly allowance from his family back home. There would be no need for jobs, and they could live in his nice apartment and easily afford drugs. What could be better?

But when they were released from Hazelton, Alexander choose to move—alone—to a sober house in St. Paul. One day, he called me to give me the news that he had been elected president of the house. He was proud, and I was thrilled for him. It was a minor achievement, but a real one, and I took it as a sign that he would make it. It took fully a year for him to give up drugs entirely. As he described it, he finally had a clear and sudden realization that he could no longer lie, cheat, and steal as he had done for so long. He told a friend who was also struggling to get sober that at last he knew he couldn't live like that any longer. The friend was supportive, and helped him clear the final hurdle, and Alexander's desperate desire to drink and use drugs disappeared.

Perhaps the best thing that happened during that time in Saint Paul was that Alexander got a job as an electrician's apprentice. Under other circumstances, I might have wanted him to get a more distinguished job, but I was overjoyed. I knew that learning a trade would ultimately give him huge self-confidence—and it did. I went to visit him and discovered that he had transformed his dingy little apartment into a delightful home for himself. He had installed beautiful lighting in the kitchen, acquired very nice furniture for the living room, and had built a wall of shelves for books. He welcomed me warmly, and my time with him filled me with hope I had not dared have for a long time.

When Robin's trial in Washington was over, he, Nancy, and Matthew went back to their apartment in Arcata. He and Nancy both enrolled in classes at College of the Redwoods, a community college in Eureka, and Nancy continued the work she loved at Mad Rivers Gardens in Arcata. She was a dedicated gardener and was happiest when she was tending plants. She helped Robin from time to time with his growing operations, but she was not really involved in the marijuana business. Her life was centered around caring for Matthew, working at the greenhouse and nursery, and taking her classes. She was stretched too thin, as many young mothers are, and increasingly she longed for a quiet, bucolic life much more like the one she had known growing up in Rhode Island, where her parents raised horses.

The big money Robin was making wasn't enough for Nancy to stay with him, and eventually she left—taking Matthew with her. I had urged Robin to marry Nancy—whom I had always loved—many times during the preceding years, but marriage was something he did not want or perhaps felt that he was not suited to. What had once been an idyllic relationship between two flower children disintegrated into acrimony, anger, and a protracted fight over the custody of Matthew.

Not long after Nancy left, Robin—still as charismatic as ever despite the injury to his foot and his drug addiction—began a relationship with a woman named Amy Forman who had grown up Humboldt. Amy was not brilliantly educated but she was kind and good-hearted and she adored Robin. She had a son named Eli, who was about Matthew's age, and they moved to a stunning house with six acres or so of lawn on a cliff fifty feet above the rocky Pacific shore. Because of the bags full of cash he was making as a marijuana farmer, Robin could afford a lifestyle he had never known before. He continued to surf as often as he liked. He loved lavishing attention on Matthew, who was with him often, and Matthew and Eli—who shared a bedroom—became as close as brothers. Robin built an indoor skateboarding park with some of the money the marijuana generated and that needed to be spent rather than simply buried. He loved the idea that local kids would have a safe place to hang out. He didn't bother to charge for its use, and he became a passionate skateboarder himself despite his injured foot.

But the laid-back hippie vibe that had initially had such a powerful allure for Robin was disappearing. Humboldt was becoming "Scumboldt," many people agreed. Reggae and the light-hearted, psychedelic music of the Grateful Dead were being replaced by gangster rap—music that had its roots in the criminal underworld of cities like New York, Philadelphia, Oakland, and Los Angeles. It was music that celebrated lawlessness and violence. Marijuana growers in far northern California increasingly used an arsenal of weapons to defend their valuable crops against people who traveled up from the south intent on raiding remote pot fields and indoor operations. And locally renowned "Snake Bite Robin" became "Pistol Robin" when his attraction to firearms became one of the central elements of his life.

Gangbangers from California's cities brought cocaine, crack, and heroin with them, and hard drugs became as widespread as pot in Humboldt County. Workers who trimmed the precious "buds" on acres of mature marijuana plants increasingly used cocaine as a way to make their otherwise grindingly boring work fly by, and it was common for both growers and these hired hands to carry pistols in their belts and rifles in their pickups.

When Chris Kelly, Robin's old friend from Baltimore, visited he was amazed by how much things had changed up among the redwoods. Chris was in the marijuana business himself, but he had never smoked a joint or even drunk a beer in his life. He was fiercely loyal to Robin, and now he worried about Robin's safety. He remembers accompanying him to a house whose windows were heavily curtained and finding a frightening guy inside the darkened house who was so stoned on *something* that he was literally chewing his fingers. Robin and the guy filled a five-gallon bucket with water, then submerged bottles filled with crack smoke into the water and used a tube to suck out the concentrated smoke while each man helped hold the other upside down. This "inverted bong hit" was a way to get a sudden and enormously powerful hit of crack, and it appeared to Chris that, for Robin, getting high this way was not at all out of the ordinary.

But the thing that astounded Chris that afternoon was the moment when the owner of the house pulled back a sliding panel in a wall to expose literally *hundreds* of guns—pistols, rifles, assault weapons of all makes and calibers—more firearms than Chris imagined could ever be stockpiled in a single place. Chris also saw plastic buckets filled with what appeared to be ball bearings, and at last he understood *why* they had come to the house. The guy manufactured sound suppressors, or "silencers," in his garage and Robin was purchasing a large quantity of them for his own weapons.

During a phone conversation with Chris sometime later, Robin reminded him of their visit to the guy's house and was excited to share the news that he was back in business supplying silencers to narco-traffickers in Mexico. There was a huge demand for them among Mexican criminals, Robin told him, and the income this new export business produced was tremendous.

Chris's devotion to his friend Robin, and his desire to see him set his life on a new track, led him to agree to join me on a trip to California when I received word that Robin had been admitted to a Eureka detox center and placed on a seventy-two-hour hold. It was not clear to us who had alerted authorities to Robin's crisis, but he confessed after being admitted that he had spent several days consuming nothing but crack cocaine, oxycontin, and morphine—and he was in terrible shape.

Things were going from bad to worse. Robin had confided to Chris by telephone before our arrival that recently one of his employees at his underground growing facility had pulled a pistol and shot and killed another employee during an argument. Robin was not at the site at the time, but he rushed there when he got the news. He panicked and did the only thing he could think to do—mounting his backhoe and burying the body as quickly as he could. He also informed the murderer that he would leave the area immediately and would travel far away and never return if he did not want to suffer a similar fate.

Robin realized after the fact that simply burying the body was not likely to end the matter, and the shock and worry helped him slide into an ever-deeper hole. By telephone, he had asked Chris if he would bring him some China gold heroin from Baltimore when he returned, but Chris told to his friend that he was simply flying out to be with him. He would *not* be bringing any heroin along.

On March 1, 2004, Chris and I flew together to Sacramento, where we stayed with my sister Mary. We sent word to Robin that we were nearby and that we hoped he would join us. Amy offered to keep Robin's beloved pit bull, Cowboy, and said she would ensure that Robin made the short flight to Sacramento the following day. We hoped that Chris could persuade Robin to go straight, but Robin didn't arrive until several days later. When he finally got there and Chris told him he was wasting his life and risking an early death, Robin simply told Chris he was wrong. He was fine, he said. His foot was okay, his life with Amy, Eli, and Matthew was good, and he still had plenty of money.

That statement didn't square with what Robin had told me earlier about being $10,000 behind in monthly rent for the land on which the skateboard park sat, but Robin was adamant. He was fine. Yet he *did* have a medical condition that needed to be resolved. As he explained it, some sort of parasite was living under the skin of his arms. This microscopic creature was known as "the portal of evil," he said, and the itching and burning it caused was unbearable.

The dermatologist in Eureka I persuaded Robin to see told him that the test he performed was normal but suggested that the itching might be caused by scabies, a tiny parasitic mite that burrows under the skin and causes an allergic reaction. He explained that a topical cream would readily kill the mites, but Robin was suspicious. He was convinced he knew better, and that the dermatologist was trying to trick him.

I didn't know at the time that Robin's terribly itchy arms were symptoms of a condition known as "cocaine psychosis," a disorder characterized by hallucinations, paranoia, delirium, and anxiety. Heavy cocaine users are often convinced that something has invaded their body—or that someone has implanted a toxic invader of some kind. Whatever the cause, Robin was in terrible shape, so next I suggested that we go together to the Mayo Clinic in Rochester, Minnesota, where surely the problem could be solved. I was surprised when he agreed, and I took his quick agreement to go as a sign that he was really in agony.

On the drive from the Minneapolis-Saint Paul airport to Rochester, Robin talked loudly, nonstop, and quite wildly. He was about to move to Barbados, he said, where he would grow psychedelic mushrooms and sell them to cruise ships. He was also in the midst of developing a big luxury resort property in Costa Rica, and he told me he missed the days back when he was Peter Pan. We spent the night in an awful fleabag inn in Rochester, and the next day Robin received a thorough examination before he was informed that there was absolutely nothing wrong with his skin. The Mayo Clinic's charge for the consultation was $1,500, and I paid it. Robin returned to northern California even more convinced that physicians were conspiring to kill him.

I didn't visit Alexander on that short trip to Minnesota, but Robin did. Neither had ever been eager to spent time with the other, and I worried a bit that the very different places in which they currently found themselves might make matters worse for Robin or Alexander or both of them. But I also took it as a hopeful sign that Robin wanted to see his older brother. Perhaps he hoped to learn from him how he could get straight himself. If Alexander had successfully turned his life around, perhaps Robin believed he could do the same.

Ann did not return to Minnesota. She and Alexander did not split up, but they drifted apart and ultimately found other partners. Alexander began to date other women in time; he became a serious bicyclist, getting himself into excellent physical shape, and he now took sober living very seriously.

Perhaps the best thing that happened to him after he turned his life around was that he was offered a job by Dr. James Fearing, protégé of addiction intervention pioneer Dr. Vernon Johnson. An Episcopal priest and recovering alcoholic himself, Johnson had become renowned for his highly effective intervention model, one embraced by Dr. Fearing that focused on "tough love" and the belief that addictions destroy whole families rather than just the individual addicts. When Dr. Fearing, only in his forties, died of cancer in 2002, Alexander was asked to continue his work.

Soon after Dr. Fearing's death, together with Robert Kovack—now a vice-president of business development at Hazelton—Alexander founded Addiction Recovery Services, the nation's first behavioral-health crisis consulting company. ARS's work focused on implementing formal relationships for crisis-call management, intervention, and case management with some of the leading treatment centers in the U.S., including Hazelden, Menninger, Silver Hill, and Sierra Tucson. A few years later, Alexander and Kovack would co-author a book for families devastated by a loved one's addiction.

ARS eventually became ARS-Health, which is by now the national leader in behavioral health disease management and crisis consulting. Alexander focused his work on helping individuals, families, and organizations overcome behavioral health challenges related not only to chemical dependency, but also eating disorders and mental-health issues. He met and ultimately married a lovely Minnesota woman named Leslie, who is now the CEO of ARS-Health. In 2011 they had a daughter they named Morgan and a son named Anthony in 2015.

Alexander had never had a strong emotional connection to me. That did not change as he began to be successful, and he called me only on rare occasions. I was proud of him, the life he had created for himself out of his personal crisis, and the career he built that was focused on helping others. But although Robin was well enough to attend his brother's wedding—calling him "Alex" when he spoke warmly about him at the reception, as virtually no one else did or does—the first decade of the new century was a very difficult one for my youngest son, the one who remained an addict.

Scumboldt

Robin was an addict. But he was still a farmer, a businessman, someone whose livelihood, and even his life were increasingly at risk in Humboldt County. It was a dangerous place, and Robin's once-happy life there was gone.

At the height of his success, he farmed marijuana on four properties, earning a profit of more than $600,000 a year. He lived in a house on six acres that overlooked the Pacific Ocean. He had a beautiful girlfriend and a son he adored. He worked hard but he also found time to surf almost every day. He built a skatepark for local kids and was a respected member of Humboldt's outlaw pot-growing community. But when his good life collapsed, it did so quickly.

In 1983, the Campaign Against Marijuana Planting—also known as CAMP—had been created as a multi-agency task force overseen by the California Department of Justice, its goal the eradication of illegal marijuana growing and trafficking throughout California. CAMP raids on marijuana crops increased every season, and for growers like Robin, gangsters were no longer their only enemies.

It was as if Humboldt, Mendocino, and Trinity counties had been invaded by an army. Helicopters flew overhead daily looking for illegal grows, which law-enforcement officers would destroy by burning them when they found them. The CAMP operation drove growers farther into the woods, into abandoned buildings, and literally underground. It was war, and growers, gangsters, and federal and state officers all possessed the weapons of war that made Humboldt and neighboring counties very dangerous places to be. So many people were shot or simply disappeared unaccountably in the Rancho Sequoia area of southeastern Humboldt County that it became renowned as "Murder Mountain."

As Robin remembers, the homicide at his underground bunker was the time when everything began to crash around him. The murdered man had been a friend of his, and their two sons had played together. For two years following his death, Robin supported the man's family, and he successfully evaded the sheriff's department's regular inquiries about what Robin knew about the dead man's disappearance. In the end, he and the local cops made a deal. He would show them the location of the buried body, and, in return, Robin would not be charged with being an accessory to murder after the fact.

Sometime later, Robin gave a prized Glock pistol to another friend who told him he really needed it. Robin presumed the man wanted it for protection, and he was devastated when five days later the friend used it to commit suicide.

Amy left him. He was only able see Matthew on a schedule approved by Nancy—and Robin hated how seldom he saw his son. Then, on March 31, 2002—Easter Sunday—gangsters from Los Angeles descended on his Trinidad home, hoping to steal a large stash of marijuana they had been told by an informer was in Robin's possession. The gang, led by a former Navy Seal, had robbed Robin before, but this time he was shocked—and terrified—that they had found his home and were demanding drugs he simply didn't have.

Robin remembers how calm the gang leader was when he found him inside his house, how he never raised his voice or appeared agitated in any way, but he was adamant: he wanted the three hundred pounds of sale-ready marijuana he *knew* Robin had there; he wanted the $300,000 stockpile of weapons he had been told Robin had stashed, and he wanted everything *now*. Robin gave the guy all the cash he had, gave him a couple of jars of pot he kept under his bed. He tried to explain that he would have to be insane to store his product and his weapons at his home. But the gangbanger wouldn't believe him. He sat eight-year-old Matthew—who was visiting his father that weekend—down in front of Robin and pressed the barrel of a .45 caliber pistol to the boy's forehead, telling Robin he would kill his son if he did not produce the pot and the weapons.

Robin was desperate. He was terrified, but he couldn't produce what the man wanted—he didn't have the marijuana or the weapons. Somehow, he was finally able to convince the man holding the pistol of that fact. Matthew lived; Robin survived, but he was never the same. Despite what his precious son meant to him, he no longer cared whether he lived or died. In addition to his pot and crack cocaine addictions, he began to shoot up heroin every day as well. It was hard for me to imagine that he could live like that much longer. His injured foot was constantly infected; he was surrounded by lethal weapons and people eager to use them. His addictions now consumed him.

Robin was in crisis. He was in danger of being evicted from a house he rented in McKinleyville, north of Arcata, and from a property farther north in the Bald Hills area where he grew pot. He owed thousands of dollars in rent for the skateboard park, and his income from growing had dropped dramatically. When California voters approved medical marijuana in 1996, the price of illegal marijuana plummeted. Robin had not gone through the process of becoming a licensed grower, and now could not compete with those who had.

When Alexander and his friend Chris Hedrington—who operated halfway houses for addicts in Colorado—visited Robin, they were shocked by what they found. Robin's head was shaved; he had no eyebrows or eyelashes, and his teeth had turned brown. He told them he had only about $150 to his name but was adamant that things would turn around for him financially when he sold a piece of property he owned near the Klamath River.

I was proud of Alexander for travelling to northern California in hopes that he could help his brother. This kind of intervention was his work, of course, and I was optimistic that Robin would listen to his older brother and agree to get the help he needed.

Robin liked his life in beautiful northern California, he told Chris and his brother. The only thing he would change, he said, would be to find a way to spend more time with Matthew. But because of Robin's drug use, Nancy was petitioning the court to forbid *any* contact between father and son. Alexander was not optimistic, but somehow before he and his friend departed, they had convinced Robin to get in-patient treatment at Sierra Tucson, a well-known addiction treatment center in Arizona, a center that Alexander thought was a good fit for his brother.

Robin flew to Arizona and checked himself into Sierra Tucson on May 5, 2006. I was in Washington. Amy's mother called to tell me he had made the decision to go, but she also shared her perception that he looked "just awful." I telephoned Nancy, who still lived in Humboldt County. She said Robin had not called for several weeks to ask if he could see Matthew. Both bits of information worried me all the more about Robin's poor condition.

When he called me soon thereafter asking if I would fly to Arizona for "Family Week" at Sierra Tucson, I agreed. But when I arrived, I almost did not recognize him. I found him leaning against a corner in a kind of daze. He wore a little black hat to cover his bald head. He still had no eyebrows or eyelashes, and at first I took him for a Los Angeles gangster.

In the cafeteria where we talked, Robin exploded, accusing me of "fixing it" so he could not see his son, working when he was young instead of being a stay-at-home mom, "attending cocktail parties" as he was growing up, and any number of supposed atrocities. In a group meeting the following day, I spoke about how Robin had recently been found with a loaded Glock and a note beside him, evidence that he intended to kill himself, but according to Robin, I was at fault because when I received this news in faraway Washington, I had called the police. He told the other addicts and family members present that I never supported him and had constantly had him tested because I thought he was "crazy." It seemed that both Robin and I were both damaged beyond repair.

When Sierra Tucson caregivers recommended long-term care for Robin, he declined. He said all he needed was to see his son and his pit bulls and get back to work, but he did promise to attend Alcoholics Anonymous meetings and regularly see a psychiatrist in Arcata. He left, and I flew home to Washington.

About a month later, I spoke with Nancy again and she reported that Robin had no job, no car, and no phone. She had told Robin that unless he at least had a mobile phone so that Matthew could call if he needed her, she would not allow him to see Matthew unless she was present. She shared that Robin had also gotten drunk recently and local police had found him sitting on a street corner and had taken him to the "drunk tank" to sober up overnight.

When Robin finally did get a mobile phone, Nancy relented and agreed that Robin could take Matthew for pizza and a movie. She told me that when she picked up Matthew after their time together, she was relieved to see that although he was still wearing low-hanging, baggy pants, at least he wasn't dressed in his usual gangster garb—a baseball cap worn sideways, a white "wife-beater" T-shirt, and heavy chains.

In May 2007, I received a call from Robin's father John telling me that Robin had been arrested for felony possession of heroin. Police had initially stopped Robin as he walked because his dog was off-leash, but when the cops saw the needle-tracks on his arms they took him into custody and searched the house where he was staying—finding enough heroin, OxyContin, and paraphernalia that it appeared they were intended for sale.

John posted bond and Robin was released from jail. Alexander arranged for Justin Diehl, an associate at his company, to fly to Humboldt and escort Robin to Hazelden's Newberg, Oregon treatment center. But before they left for Oregon, Robin jumped out the bathroom window of his drug-addicted lawyer's house and disappeared. He had gone "home" to get heroin, of course, but according to Robin, he had just wanted to "gather some clothes." The following day, when I spoke with Robin by phone, he confessed that he "needed heroin" right now, largely because Amy had left him, and the loss was hard to bear. Justin Diehl and Robin's friend and lawyer Elaine Profant-Turner finally succeeded in getting Robin on an airplane—accompanied by Diehl—and the two men made it to Hazelden Newberg, about forty-five minutes southwest of Portland, without another incident.

A week later, I spoke by phone with Joann Murphy, Robin's counselor at Hazelden Newberg, and she was clearly getting to know my son. "Robin gets by on charm," she told me. "He's the kind of guy who could sell freezers to Eskimos." In that same conversation, she told me that Robin's life lacked structure, and that he needed to address the role of his father in his life. From what she had learned so far, she said, John had never disciplined Robin in any way throughout his life, and had always bailed him out of whatever trouble—large or small—he was in. The result was that Robin believed he was "entitled" and that he really didn't need to be responsible for his behavior—trusting that his father would make the trouble go away and not be angry with him.

About a week later, I got a call from Sally, John's wife, who was very angry with me. Apparently, Joann or someone else at Hazelden Newberg had shared that perspective with John himself, and he presumed that surely I was responsible. Sally went on at length about what a good father her husband was now and had always been, and how *I* was the problem. "No wonder your kids are so fucked up," she yelled before she slammed down the phone.

A few hours later, Sally called again to apologize—which I appreciated—and to tell me that she and John had decided to go to Oregon for a "Family Week," much like the one I had attended at Sierra Tucson. But before they could begin their trip, Robin suggested to both his father and me that the best place for him to recover was likely either Ocean Recovery or Morningside, both centers located in Newport Beach, where the surfing was good.

Joann Murphy called me from Hazelden Newberg, frustrated that Robin seemed determined to direct his own care and insistent that it was time for him to grow up and take his circumstances seriously. When I spoke with Robin, he reminded me that his brother had been a "hardcore" heroin user for four years and now was fine. In his case, he insisted, he really wasn't much of a heroin user. He was a pot smoker and was not sick. He had just gotten "caught int the wrong room at the wrong time." He had entirely forgotten that he had told me the truth just a few days before.

On June 27, John called to me that Robin was "ensconced" at Morningside in Newport Beach. He and Robin had reached an agreement, he said. John would pay for Robin's three-month stay at Morningside and have his surfboard delivered there, and Robin in turn promised to focus intently on getting well.

Morningside was a disaster—so bad that John and I were in utter agreement for the first time in many years that he was wasting his money, and Robin could not recover in a playground for spoiled rich kids. On September 12, Robin secured a pass that allowed him to leave the Morningside campus for a few hours. While he was away, he scored some OxyContin and got high. The opioid was found in a urine sample, and Morningside staffers escorted him to a local detox facility. A week later, Robin was officially released, and he returned immediately to Humboldt. He said he just needed a job and to see his son. He would be fine.

After the Shooting

In the summer of 2008, Robin traveled south to Tulare County on the western edge of California's Central Valley. His dream life in Humboldt had crashed down around him. He had been admitted to three addiction treatment centers and had left or been asked to leave all three. His chronic money troubles continued, and he opted to go to work with his friend D.J., who grew marijuana north of the tiny town of Three Rivers, between Visalia and the entrance to Sequoia National Park.

On July 24, a Thursday, Robin was driving alone when he stopped at a makeshift parking lot and made the short hike down to a beautiful natural swimming hole at the base of Cherry Falls on the North Fork of the Kaweah River. Following his swim, he hiked back up to the parking lot, where he saw three or four gangbangers—from Los Angeles, he guessed—who appeared to be in their forties surrounding a Jeep filled with teenage girls, and he didn't like what he saw.

He was wearing flip-flops, a T-shirt, and quick-dry shorts and wasn't carrying a weapon. He walked up to the group of men and said, "Dude, these girls are like sixteen. I mean, come on. There's a cardinal rule here. It's like written in the California gangsters rule book and underlined three times. You don't mess with girls younger than your kids."

When one of the men told Robin this was none of his fucking business, Robin did not back down. The guy was aggressive; Robin was, too. Robin had been working hard in the marijuana fields and was in good shape and was sure he could take the guy, if he had to. "Okay. Then let's get down, punk," he said, stepping closer to the man—who suddenly pulled out a .38 caliber pistol, pointed it at him and asked, "You think I'm a punk now?"

"Dude, that's a punk move right there, for sure," Robin responded, and the man shot him three times in the chest at point-blank range.

Robin fell to the dirt, as everyone scattered. D.J. and his girlfriend Crissy, whose house and growing operation were close by, heard his cries for help and rushed to him. They got Robin into their big diesel pickup truck; Crissy pressed her hands hard against Robin's chest, but she couldn't stop the bleeding and the seat got very wet. Robin begged for D.J. to drive faster, but the roads twisted and turned, and D.J. shouted that if he drove any faster they *all* would die. Crissy poured a bottle of liquid OxyContin down Robin's throat, which dramatically lowered his blood pressure and kept much of his blood inside his abdomen and likely kept him alive. About forty-five minutes passed before they finally reached the Visalia hospital, and by the time they were out of the mountains Robin had begun to ebb in and out of consciousness.

Robin had a spotty memory of the next couple of weeks, and no memory at all of much that occurred. Some of what he believed truly happened almost certainly did not. He remembered D.J. and Crissy walking him into the hospital's emergency room, for example, but the people at the hospital were adamant when they told me that Robin had stumbled into the emergency room on his own and that the truck that dropped him off had sped away. Robin recounted that the surgery that saved his life took place at one o'clock in the morning, but he was shot on a hot July afternoon, and the trip down into central Visalia did not take ten or eleven hours—although perhaps it felt to him like it did. And he remembered that he had been unconscious for nine days following the surgery, but he spoke with me just a couple of days after he was shot.

Many years later, Robin explained that when he told Visalia police detective Steven Kennedy that he did not know who shot him it was true—at the time. He later did learn who had shot him. But even if he had known, he said, he would not have identified the shooter. "We don't snitch," he said. "If I ended up in a California state prison and word got out that I was a snitch, I'd be dead in a day." That, too, was the reason he told Kennedy he did not know who had driven him to the hospital. He did not want to involve D.J. or Crissy in the shooting investigation in any way. They were not legal growers, and they did not need cops breathing down their necks.

Robin had a clear memory of one of his surgeons visiting him in his hospital room and telling him that, while Robin was on the operating table, the surgeon did not expect to see him alive again. Robin remembered, too, the day when a burly nurse lifted him out of bed and sat him in a wheelchair for the first time since the shooting and his surgery, then walked away. The transfer caused the most intense pain he had ever experienced, he told me, because his internal organs hadn't settled back into place. He was helpless and simply had to endure the torture, but it was so overwhelming that he thought the pain alone might kill him.

Robin remembered that he spent six weeks in the Visalia hospital, but he was there just over three weeks, in fact. In Robin's mind, he recovered at home with me in Washington for half a year, but actually, he went back to California after only two months. He did not remember thanking me for saving his life as he left.

I had presumed that Robin would return to Humboldt County and the outlaw life he lived there when he reached California. I was certain he wouldn't return to the area where he had been shot, and I was surprised to find out that he had gone to Los Angeles. Someone he knew in the drug business had offered him his large, empty house. The key was hidden behind a brick near the front door, the friend explained, and Robin holed up there in a small room on the first floor. But his pain remained intense enough that before he settled in he went out and scored a gram of heroin. The physician-prescribed fentanyl patches he had brought with him from Washington weren't strong enough to block the pain. He was desperate and shooting heroin—something with which he already had lots of experience—seemed to be his only option.

But he could barely get out of bed, and he realized that he was going to have to get some help. He reached the owner of the house by telephone, explained his pain and predicament, and before long a woman named Maija James came to the door—someone who would fall in love with him as she began to care for him. Maija and I began to communicate regularly by email and telephone calls—and I was grateful to hear from her so often.

Robin learned during the year he spent recovering in Los Angeles, a city he had always hated, that the man who shot him was part of the TKO Crew, a Mexican American gang whose 1980s roots were in "tagging"—graffiti vandalism—but it was a gang that had grown very violent in the 1990s. The man who had shot him, he now knew, had moved to Nevada, where state law allowed him to legally marry his sixteen-year-old girlfriend. Robin knew that the guy dropped off his teenage wife every afternoon at the Las Vegas strip club where she worked, and he fantasized about quietly exacting revenge against the gangbanger who had tried to kill him. "I thought about it an awful lot," he said. "He's alive. I know he's alive. If I wanted to snitch on him, what would he get? Six years for attempted murder or something like that? No. Not doing that. But he doesn't deserve to live."

While Robin slowly recovered in Los Angeles with the help of Maija's constant care, he also had plenty of time to discover who was responsible for the Easter raid on his house on the Humboldt County coast two years before—another L.A. gangster whom Robin also believed did not deserve to live. But it wasn't the man who had held the pistol to his son Matthew's head whom Robin wanted dead. Instead, it was the gang leader who had ordered the assault from hundreds of miles away. He knew where the gang leader lived, knew what time of day he liked to step out onto the balcony of his apartment to smoke. When I asked if Robin was certain this guy was still alive, he chillingly replied, "We don't need to talk about him."

Maija was Latvian, and very devoted to her family. Her father was Gundars Rudzitis, a professor emeritus of geography at the University of Idaho who had also taught at Boston University and the University of Texas. He had been a Fulbright scholar and was the author of *The Ongoing Transformation of the American West* and *Wilderness and the Changing American West*. Maija was a writer, too, and, like her father, rather brilliant. She was a voracious reader and she loved to paint. She was always interesting and charming, but Maija had demons. She was a mean and obnoxious drunk—something I saw first-hand when Maija drank heavily at my niece's house in Sacramento when and Robin came for dinner. He had begged her not to drink, but she did anyway. She became argumentative, rude, and obnoxious. Robin was helpless to stop her and was angry at her and embarrassed by her behavior. But she loved Robin, and he loved her too, and he was close to her brother Erik Leons as well.

When Robin—whom Maija like to call "Petal" for reasons she never explained—was well enough after about a year in Los Angeles, he was eager to return to Humboldt County on the Oregon border. And Maija moved with him. By then, our irregular exchange of email messages had matured into a steady pen-pal relationship and Maija often commented in long and sometimes rambling messages to me that I mattered enormously to her because I was the woman who had brought Robin into the world. "I love your son Very Much, Eliza," she wrote, and it was clear that she did.

Up in Humboldt, Maija found herself in a community of marijuana growers whose operations had become quasi-legal. "I will write you more extensively later," she wrote in September 2010,

> although I can say that I very much like the other principal members of Robin's grower group up here, Chris & Scott. And the scene is extremely organized & seems for the most part very open & congenial between everyone involved. It is quite beautiful also where Robin has situated his RV & communal outdoor quarters, which he has located just above his lot of plants, up above the rest, which looks out across the valleys & bare hills and the small cabin below where they have their meals. . . . I have always been around those who use weed yet am not "hip" to any of it—so this has been a very interesting time. . . . I hope that even if Robin's and my lifestyles cannot completely sync up that he and I will Never part from the core connections we have found together—yet as I said, I am just trying to keep my head in a reasonable arena and leave space for time and life to fill in the unknown cracks, so to speak.

Maija and Robin grew close enough that he confessed to her the terrible nightmares that were common to him, and she, in turn, shared that with me, telling me that he often cried and shouted in his sleep. Robin's past was a deeply troubled and violent one, she knew, and Maija did her best to help him imagine a different life. "He has been mentioning ever since the shooting and seeing how wonderful it was that the doctors & nurses were truly helping people that he wishes he was doing something that helped others," she wrote. "But when he's feeling low and has the blues, he laments that he is still 'just a drug-dealer.'"

By October of that year, Maija had determined that she and Robin could not endure as a couple and she had returned to Los Angeles, although they remained in close touch. She understood that somehow she and Robin could only be "best friends" and that they would not have a future as lovers. From Los Angeles, she wrote that her brother Erik strongly believed that Robin survived the shooting "for a reason," yet neither Erik nor Maija—nor Robin, most importantly of all—knew what that reason was. "He truly should deep down realize that there is a purpose for him to be for the most part healthy again, and that he still has an important life ahead of him—if he chooses to have it," she wrote.

On one of last occasions when Maija sent me email, she wrote, "Robin has always given and does give me constant support, and I hope he will always allow me to remain close enough to him to be able to return his love and support and always show him my appreciation by being as much behind him as is humanly possible. Thank you so much for everything. Life is certainly emotional and unpredictable. Love to you, dear Eliza."

Robin had lived with little more than an often-infected and seriously damaged right foot for many years. And he had come extremely close to dying when he was shot in the chest in the summer of 2008. Over time, he physically recovered remarkably well. By now was able to work long and taxing days in the marijuana gardens. He remained in constant pain, however, and the pain fueled his need for heroin and other drugs. I'm also sure that his addictions exacerbated the depression he sank into when he began to try to contend with a series of difficult losses that all too often came his way.

Beginning not long after Robin returned to northern California, his close friend "Tro" Trowbridge accidentally shot himself and died. His friend Jay Marinaccio had a bicycle accident in San Diego that left him paralyzed and confined to a wheelchair. Robin continued to be haunted by having buried his longtime employee and friend Rick Shin following his murder some years before. His former partner Nancy increasingly kept their son Matthew away from him and what she saw as his father's terrible influence. Then she and Matthew moved to Rhode Island with Nancy's new husband Dean Viseth, so Robin almost never saw his son.

Robin once had money. He owned a grand house overlooking the Pacific, had successful—if mostly illegal—businesses, vehicles, and friends who loved him. But he had lost—or was losing—it all. By 2012, he was living in a travel trailer without utilities on a large marijuana farm owned by his old friend Chris

Kelly. When the concerns of land-use code-enforcement officers led to a search of the trailer by Humboldt County Sheriff's deputies, they found a cache of guns and Oxycontin pills in addition to the vast acreage of illegal cannabis plants. Robin was charged with three felonies—illegal plant cultivation, possession of lethal weapons while committing a drug offense, and possession of narcotics and controlled substances. It was the first time he had been arrested since his marijuana bust in San Diego back in 1992. But it would not be his last.

Robin was scheduled to come to Washington to visit me and his father and stepmother Sally for Christmas in 2016 when I received a phone call from him saying, "I'm in trouble." He had been arrested at the San Francisco airport for felony possession of marijuana intended for sale. Cannabis use for medicinal purposes was legal in California by then and, of course, Robin had become a medical marijuana patient. He contended that, as a patient, the law allowed him to legally possess ten pounds of pot, but he was arrested, nonetheless. His marijuana was confiscated, and he was required to post a $20,000 bond—paid for by his father. At trial, Robin accepted a plea bargain and pleaded guilty to a misdemeanor prior to being sentenced to eighteen months' probation.

Less than a month later—on the cold and dark day when Donald Trump was inaugurated as president of the United States just a couple of miles from my home—I received a telephone call from Crystal Herren, Robin's current girlfriend, telling me that he was in the intensive care unit at Alta Bates Summit Medical Center in Berkeley because he had suffered what the doctors were calling grand mal seizures the previous night. According to Crystal, he had several seizures in a row—one lasting at least twenty minutes.

Just as I had eight and a half years before, when I received the news that Robin likely was hospitalized in Visalia, I got on a plane the following day and flew to California. From the San Francisco airport, I called the hospital and learned that Robin already had been discharged, and it was likely that he had gone to the warehouse where he and Crystal lived and worked. I got a taxi and gave the driver the warehouse's Oakland address. It seemed like we drove for hours before we reached the alley that led to the warehouse, which was surrounded by a high wire fence. It was a bad part of the city; it had begun to rain, and the sky had turned dark, and—afraid for his safety if not for mine—the driver refused to take me to the warehouse's door.

I was appalled. I gave him a hundred-dollar bill, got my small bag, and walked down the darkening alley, opened the gate in the high chain-link fence and saw a man who turned out to be Crystal's brother. He asked me if I was Robin's mother. I told him I was, and he pointed toward a closed door. When I knocked at the warehouse door, Crystal opened it. She let me in, then quickly left.

The interior of the place was dark and ugly. It was windowless and dirty. I saw Robin sitting slumped on a broken-down sofa. When I asked how he was, he told me he was weak but felt okay, saying that doctors at the hospital had put him on an anticonvulsant called Keppra and had told him he was not allowed to drive. When I asked for the bathroom, Robin got up, struggled to get his balance in a way that frightened me, then led me outside and around the corner of the building to a toilet room where I saw two disgusting toilets that looked like they had never been cleaned.

When I returned to Robin, I told him I would take him to dinner. But a suspicious-looking group of men were loitering in front of the first restaurant we walked to. He knew another place, and it was dismal, but we ate there anyway. When I asked, he matter-of-factly said that yes, the doctors at Summit Medical had told him heavy drug use often led to seizure disorders. After dinner, although his balance remained poor, he walked me a few blocks to a motel he had chosen for me—a place where cars came into the parking lot, stayed a few minutes, then drove away throughout the night.

The next morning, I invited Robin to come to the motel and take a shower in "my nice, clean white bathroom." He did and said it was exactly what he needed. He was still weak but was able to walk to a good nearby restaurant where we had delicious Swedish pancakes. Then we went to the Oakland Museum where he was fascinated by an exhibit on beekeeping. That afternoon, my niece Becky and her husband picked me up and took me to their friend's house up in the Oakland Hills for dinner and an overnight stay. Robin met us at their house the following day, and he seemed to continue to feel better—improved enough that I felt comfortable getting on a flight that afternoon that took me home to Washington.

There were moments in that grim era when Robin seemed to be at a desperately low ebb. But he demonstrated, nonetheless, that he longed for a different life. Although he was often homeless, and his addictions continued to drag him into an abyss, from time-to-time Robin rallied. He traveled several times with his father and stepmother Sally to Costa Rica and Barbados, and he was good about visiting me in Washington and Jack and Sally in nearby Lexington, Virginia at Christmas and Easter. He always let us know that we mattered to him, despite the fact that he was often inconsiderate, sometimes spiteful.

Six months following the night of seizures and his subsequent hospitalization in Berkeley, Robin traveled to St. Paul to visit Alexander his family and me. All of us packed up one hot summer afternoon and drove to the University Club, where Alexander and his wife Leslie were members, so we could swim. It seemed odd when Robin chose to sit at an outdoor table by himself rather than with the rest of us. Then, his head fell to his chest, and he was "asleep." I asked Alexander—who worked in the recovery business, of course—to check on his brother. I was certain that Robin had taken something that had effectively knocked him out. But Alexander ignored my comment as if he hadn't heard me.

When we later went to a park, Robin helped Alexander hang a huge hammock between trees to make a kind of fort that Alexander's daughter Morgan and son Tommy thought was amazing. Everyone was happy, and for a few hours at least we seemed to be a normal family.

At Christmastime that year, Robin and his girlfriend Crystal flew to the East Coast. They briefly visited Robin's son Matthew—an adult by now who lived in New York City—then traveled south to be with Robin's stepmother Sally and his father, who was seriously ill with Lewy body disease. They spent most of their time at John and Sally's farm, but they did drive into the city to have dinner with me one evening. We had dinner at my apartment. We didn't quarrel or exchange cross words, but neither did our time together feel like a special occasion. They left soon after dinner because they had left their two small dogs in a nearby hotel room. And on December 28, they went back to California.

John died thirty-six days later. He was eighty-six years old and had battled Lewy body dementia for a long time. His obituary in *The Washington Post* assured those who read it that his illness "did not rob him of his ability to read history, poetry, biography, and he continued studying his bird books and listening to music. He remained an interesting and resourceful man."

Following our divorce, John and I never became friends. We saw too many things—particularly our two sons and their well-being—too differently to be able to rebuild any kind of connection. But just as I had always developed true friendships with the women in Alexander's and Robin's lives, I had become a friend of Sally, and she and I are friends to this day.

Both boys adored their father. He was always the *fun* parent who would take them on grand international adventures, and who could be counted on to bail them out of any sticky situation. A few days after he received the news of his father's death, Robin posted on Facebook a photo of John with John's two dogs and he wrote, "My father John T Richards passed away. He lived 86 beautiful years and always lived life to its fullest. Please remember him for the kind, caring soul he always was. Service will be held for him at Christ Church, Georgetown, Washington DC Feb 22."

Despite the affluence that was John's birthright, at his death he left no financial support for Sally or either of his sons. His money was simply gone and no one—least of all me—understood where it went. Both boys grieved for their father—and Robin had to deal with another devastating loss in his life.

An Aging Junkie

By the summer of 2020, Robin had moved to a marijuana farm outside the town of Grass Valley in the Sierra Nevada foothills, roughly halfway between Sacramento and Reno. The property was owned by a guy named Rich, who was best friends with Robin's former friend, Paul Schaechter. Robin and Paul had had a serious falling out some years before because Paul was convinced that Robin was stealing from him. Robin claimed that the alleged thefts were simply part of Paul's drug-addled imagination.

I knew of Paul because I had met him, and although I knew he and Robin wanted little to do with each other these days, I also knew that Paul was closely connected to Rich, so perhaps he could tell me something—*anything*—about how Robin was doing. I had not heard from my son in months. My alarm grew with each day that passed without news, so I called Paul to see if he could tell me anything about Robin. But all Paul would say was that Robin was a crook.

Huge wildfires raged around the Grass Valley area that autumn, which compounded my worries. As far as I could tell, they were not near the farm where Robin was working, but every mother worries about her child's safety, of course, and I had plenty to worry about when it came to Robin. On October 28, I had a telephone call from his longtime friend Chris Kelly, who also was concerned about him. Chris was afraid he was in the Santa Rosa area—where the fires were destroying everything in their path—but I was able to share the information I had that Robin was actually near Grass Valley. I told Chris that I had reached out to Paul Schaechter because I knew he was close to the owner of the growing operation where Robin worked. But, so far, I had learned nothing.

About an hour after I heard from Chris, I had a call from Robin, who sounded surprisingly more clear-headed than he had in years. He told me he was fine, and that when the marijuana harvest was done he thought he would find a regular job. A "regular job" was something he had never had, but I was thrilled to hear him say it. He assured me that he hadn't used any drugs for quite a while. "Not even marijuana?" I asked. "Just every now and then," he replied.

During our conversation, I told him his son Matthew had recently visited me and that together we had driven to his step grandmother Sally's house in Lexington for an overnight stay. I told him that Sally had said she hoped he would come east for Christmas. What I didn't tell him was what Matthew had shared with me on the drive back to Washington.

The last time he had seen his father was at a dingy cafe in San Francisco when Matthew was there on business. Matthew said Robin arrived late, and when he did his face was swollen and bloody. He said he'd been in a fight at the warehouse in Oakland. He slurred his words as he spoke and didn't make sense. He wore his baggy pants low on his butt, gangster style. Matthew had been very troubled—and openly embarrassed—to see his father in that condition. He told me he was afraid someone he knew might see him and wonder why he was with this bum.

Matthew was ashamed of his father. I knew that was true, but I knew he still loved him just the same. As we continued driving, Matthew said "I'm done with him. I've got my own life to live, and seeing my dad like that was too hard for me. I'm done." But in my delight to be in touch with Robin again after so long without any news of him—and to hear him sounding so good—I simply told Robin that Matthew had asked me to promise to tell him whatever I learned about his father. Matthew might be "done" with his father, but he still wanted to know whatever I learned about him.

A couple of weeks later, Robin's friend Chris called again to ask whether I had heard from Robin once more, which I had not. I told Chris I was increasingly worried about Robin, despite his sounding so good in late October. I was worried that he was using heroin again while he was living and working in Grass Valley. "Well, there's not a lot of heroin in Grass Valley," Chris responded. "Plenty in Oakland or Washington." He meant to put my mind at ease, but I knew that Robin went to Oakland often. Did that mean that he regularly went to see his girlfriend Crystal and load up on heroin again? Were those Oakland trips simply drug runs?

While we spoke, Chris told me that during the decades Robin lived in Humboldt County, he had been a legend in the region's pot-growing world—beloved and revered. "Sharkbite" Robin. "Pistol" Robin. "People just loved him. I still do," Chris told me over the phone. But I knew this legendary character—once young and seemingly invincible, making friends almost instantly, and always able to disarm suspicions with his unique kind of charisma—had been a homeless and aging junkie for far too long for him to be to still be held in that kind of esteem.

Chris didn't like me referring to Robin as a junkie, but that's what he was. Once the king of the marijuana world, he now slept on the ground in a canvas tent, warmed by a space heater. He wore heavy Carhart work clothing to ward off the dampness and the cold. He peed and pooped wherever he could because he had no bathroom, and he took a shower only rarely—when the owner of the operation invited him to use his shower and hot water.

Less than a year following his father's death, Robin nonetheless pulled himself together enough to return to Washington at Christmas. It was the one time of year he really wanted to be here. I texted him on December 6, 2020, to tell him that I had had a car accident and had broken a vertebra. I would need a bit of extra help for a while, and I was pleased he was coming and could lend a hand. I offered to buy a round-trip ticket for him, but he declined, saying he wasn't sure yet when he would be free to travel.

Finally, he booked a last-minute, expensive flight—one I paid for—then missed the flight for a set of reasons that didn't make any sense. For twenty years, Sally, John, Robin, and sometimes one of Robin's girlfriends had a Christmas Eve tradition of eating dinner in a local restaurant then going to midnight mass at Christ Church in Georgetown. Sally had driven up from Lexington, Virginia expecting that tradition to continue even now that John was gone. And she was crushed to learn that Robin would not be able to join her when she called to tell me she had arrived in the city. Robin had not called her to apologize for his absence, or even offer her the same lame excuses he gave me.

When I woke up on Christmas morning, it was plain to see that Robin had arrived in the night. He had made up my electric folding bed for himself, and there were wrappers for Toblerone chocolates and other sweets scattered around. When he woke, I fixed us breakfast and he seemed happy to be home. Late in the morning, he said he wanted to go for a walk in the Bishop's Garden—which was near the building where I live now. My back injury kept me from joining him, but I was surprised when he hadn't returned in several hours. Sally was scheduled to have dinner with us that evening and I called him to tell him to *please* get home so his stepmother wouldn't be disappointed again.

He finally arrived, and Robin, Sally, and I—just three of us—had a lovely, quiet Christmas dinner. While she was with us, we called Alexander and his family to wish them a happy Christmas. We called Matthew, too, and Robin was sweet with him and told his son he loved him before he wished him a happy Christmas.

But as soon as Sally left, Robin took something—heroin I suppose. His skin took on an odd sheen. His face seemed to swell. He moved only in very slow motion before he lay down on my sofa and became virtually comatose, not moving a muscle, barely breathing for hours while I sat and watched him. He was still catatonic when I gave up and went to bed several hours later.

I had been retired for several years by now. Near the end of my career, I had become a partner in the Redpath, Leasure and Richards Investment Consulting Group, part of Wells Fargo Advisors. I had begun my professional life forty years before as an untrained assistant to a big producer and, at the time, I had known absolutely nothing about the world of finance.

I now lived in a lovely apartment building near the National Cathedral in northwest Washington. After a lifetime of smoking—a vice I had quit some years before—I was limited by COPD, chronic obstructive pulmonary disease, and was forced to use supplemental oxygen. I continued to see friends—men and women who had enriched my life immensely. I belonged to two book clubs and enjoyed reading books and newspapers. And I had lots of time to reflect on what I perceived as my failings as a mother and to worry about Robin's health and safety.

By June 2021, Robin had left his job at the marijuana growing operation outside Grass Valley and moved seventy-five miles north to a derelict collection of cabins and trailers in the woods outside Magalia, near the town of Paradise where, two years before, the Camp fire—one of the most destructive and deadly wildfires in U.S. history—had roared through the area and destroyed everything in its path. Magalia, just a few miles north, had been heavily damaged by the fire as well.

Amy Ogilvie, an old friend of Robin's, had urged him to come to the encampment, saying it would be a good place to establish a marijuana grow of his own. Real jobs still eluded him, and he and his girlfriend Crystal rented a single room in a dilapidated cabin in a compound of cabins owned by a local realtor named Wayne Stout.

The cabin was slowly rotting its way back into the forest. Its single bathroom did not have a door. Their room had one blacked-out window and contained only a bed, two lamps, a beat-up dresser and a large plastic cooler where they kept their food—because it would be stolen by their "housemates" if they left it in the kitchen. At least Robin wasn't living i in a tent, and now he had a toilet he could use but it was a terrible place. The cabins and trailers on the property were surrounded by abandoned vehicles and mountains of trash. Even Robin recognized that the place was all too reflective of who and what he had become. Despite the fact that a number of people paid rent to Stout, the trash, disorder, and general filth of the place made it look as if it were a homeless encampment.

By June 2021, Robin was no longer working as a cannabis grower and he and Crystal were trying without success to find a way to leave the compound and move to Oakland. Late in the afternoon of June 5, two men whom Robin did not like began to throw rocks at the cabin where he and Crystal lived.

Will Tiplick, who regularly carried a six-inch tactical knife in his belt and was often falling-down drunk, believed Robin had gotten him fired from his job as a marijuana tender. Tiplick's friend, Travis Hogan, was a paroled convict—a man whose shamrock tattoo on his chest and the swastika inked onto his shaved head identified him as a member of the Aryan Brotherhood, the oldest and most notorious racist prison gang in the United States, a gang that demands committing murder or the swearing of blood oaths of everyone who becomes a member.

Tiplick and Hogan shouted death threats at Robin and Crystal, and in an effort to stop the menacing, Robin came out of the cabin's front door with a handgun. He fired it twice into an abandoned trailer to try to scare them away. Tiplick rushed Robin and attacked him with a half-gallon whiskey bottle. The bottle hit Robin's hand and caused an accidental discharge of the gun. As Crystal filmed the encounter with her mobile phone, the two men continued their threats, then retreated. And that was the end of the incident, at least for the moment.

When Butte County sheriff's deputies arrived—at a compound they did *not* like to visit because it was known to be very dangerous—they found Tiplick lying in a gravel roadway. He had passed out drunk and wet himself. When they roused him, he told the officers he did not believe Robin had intended to hurt him or his friend Hogan.

Hogan had left the premises by now and when deputy Hugh Hooks questioned Robin, he nodded in response to some of the officer's questions but didn't actually speak. Hooks arrested Robin on the spot and took him to the Butte County jail in nearby Oroville.

At the jail, Robin was placed in a pod of about sixty men. A day later he was severely beaten by other prisoners and one of the inmates stomped on his neck. He suffered a grand mal seizure and was presumed dead before he came to consciousness and was transferred to the Enloe Medical Center in Chico, where doctors diagnosed him on June 9 with a dangerously high fever, dehydration, disorientation, COVID, hepatitis, and pneumonia. His long-injured and now hugely swollen foot was also so infected that an internist recommended its immediate amputation. Robin begged Dr. Komal Patel not to take his foot and she relented, prescribing instead a very high dose of intravenous antibiotics. And, after a few days, Robin's infection had improved enough that he was returned to the Butte County jail's medical unit.

When I got the news via a telephone call from Crystal that Robin had been arrested and was now hospitalized, I scrambled and was able to engage a local criminal-defense lawyer in Chico named Stephana Femino to defend him. When she went to the jail to meet with Robin, she found him shackled to a metal bunk, where he was lying in his own waste. He was freezing cold and didn't have a blanket or even a sweater to help keep him warm.

When Robin was arraigned, he was charged with discharging a firearm in a way that could have caused serious injury or death, shooting into an abandoned dwelling, and assault with a firearm—all serious felonies. In court, Judge Michael Deems labeled Robin a "dangerous and violent criminal." At the deputy district attorney's urging, the judge arbitrarily changed one of the charges from shooting at an abandoned trailer to shooting into an *inhabited* dwelling—despite the fact that owner Wayne Stout testified that the interior of the trailer had been so trashed at the time of the incident that only mice could live in it. Neither Tiplick nor Hogan had filed charges against Robin, and the only property damage was limited to two bullet holes in the side of the derelict trailer, but Robin now faced possible conviction on one or more of the felony counts and a very long prison sentence.

In August, Robin failed to appear at an arraignment hearing and a bench warrant was issued for his arrest. A jury trial was scheduled for early February 2022, and I flew to California to be there for him. On the morning of Wednesday, February 3, my cousin Becky—who lived in Sacramento and who had met me at the airport—and I met with a Chico lawyer named Michael Erpino. We spoke about him possibly replacing Stefana, who had been extremely slow responding to any questions I had. Erpino said Stephana was thorough, tough, well-liked, and respected by the court.

Following that meeting, we drove to the county jail in Oroville, hoping to see Robin, who had been jailed again. But we were told he had been transferred to the Oroville hospital—for reasons no one at the hospital would tell us. We were told that we could not see him because he was a prisoner. And neither could we learn anything about his condition.

By Friday, Stephana was proving to be even more difficult to speak with. She repeatedly missed meetings scheduled with me—or arrived two or three hours late. In an exchange of text messages, she explained that, so far, she had been unable to secure permission for me to see Robin in the hospital or to learn more about his condition due to HIPAA laws.

I had a call from George Veech—the son of my old friend Bud Veech. Like his father, George was a physician. He lived and practiced medicine in Portland, Oregon, and he was worried, based on what I had told him, that perhaps Robin's foot had become severely infected again. George did say that an amputation—should one become necessary—was a simple surgery that could be successfully done in a small-town hospital. Small comfort! Robin's brother Alexander texted me, suggesting that perhaps Robin was hospitalized as part of a detox plan, but that didn't sound right to me.

When we were finally able to meet and talk with Stephana, she knew nothing more about Robin's condition. But she did have news that his legal case had been refiled as a violent felony case. She told us he was now charged with shooting into an *occupied home*—and my fear skyrocketed. There was an element of insanity about the whole thing. It seemed the police simply said whatever they pleased to the judge, and without any evidence of any kind.

On Saturday, Stephana telephoned with the news that Robin was being transferred to the county jail. For many hours thereafter, we all waited outside the jail for him to be released. The light was fading in the late afternoon winter sky, and it was nerve-racking to simply stare at the so called "sallyport"—the secure enclosure where prisoners were taken in or discharged from the jail. But at last Robin walked out.

His gray hair had grown shaggy since I had last seen him. He was utterly subdued, and moved shakily, like a very old man. I asked him if he was ready to do whatever it took to turn things around and all he could mumble was, "yes." I had a paper cup with cut-up fruit leftover from my lunch. I gave it to him, and he said, "I think I'm going to cry." He hadn't seen anything like those bits of apple, orange, pineapple, and grape in a long time, and he was delighted to eat them.

We drove directly to Enloe Medical Center in Chico so he could be examined, and where I expected him to be admitted. But at about 10:00 p.m. he was released with several oral antibiotics and told to return if his infected foot worsened. Robin seemed completely detached from reality. I was terrified. But at least still had his foot. At least he was alive.

We drove from Enlow to our little rented Airbnb with a yellow door. Inside, there were two bedrooms with a bath between them. All the towels, sheets, and bed covers were pristine white. Robin acted as if he had never seen anything so grand. And for sure, everything there was very different from the place where he had lived outside Magalia.

My cousin Becky and I fed him some chicken and vegetables we had on hand. Then Robin crashed facedown onto the bed. It was my bed, but he was afraid of being alone, so I slept with him. He often woke to go to the kitchen for more food and only slept in fits and starts throughout the night.

He continued to sleep almost constantly for several days. During that time, I made a series of calls, trying to find an addiction treatment center in the area where he could be admitted. When at last he began to be awake more often, he started to converse with us as well. But he spoke in a hectoring voice, almost barking. He seemed to be pouring out his anger and talked not only about the incident at the compound, but also about the ten years—now far in the past—during which he supplied a Sinaloa drug cartel in Mexico with silencers for their guns.

On Wednesday, a week after my arrival, Becky and I drove to the collection of derelict cabins, wrecked vehicles, and abandoned trailers on Lovelock Road a few miles north of Magalia to get clothes for Robin that Crystal had packed for him.

As we drove northwest from Chico, the brown buttes that gave Butte County its name rose suddenly up from lush flatlands. The snow-covered Sierras loomed far beyond, and as we approached Paradise—or what had been the town of Paradise—we entered a sea of dead but still standing trees. A few new houses were under construction. But the foundations of burned-out homes and businesses were everywhere.

When we drew near the encampment, forests that were untouched by the Camp fire grew dark and thick. And my nervousness mounted. There was something terribly creepy about this place. I wanted to get Robin's things and get out as quickly as possible.

I thought I knew what to expect when we arrived. By now I had seen the video Crystal shot of Robin's encounter with Tiplick and Hogan, but I was shocked by the squalor of the place. We found Crystal easily enough, took the clothes she had gathered for Robin, as well as a red blanket I had given him at Christmas a few years ago. It was something he treasured, but it was sad to think of it as a middle-aged man's security blanket. Then we left.

On Thursday, February 10, 2022, Robin's new case was scheduled for a preliminary hearing. I wanted to be in court to support him, so I extended our stay in the Chico area, despite the serious toll the stress the place, the circumstances, and the worry were taking on me. It seemed as though every minute of every day demanded my *total* attention—without a moment of relief. It felt as though my blood was on fire.

Robin, Becky, and I arrived at the courthouse in Oroville at eight o'clock that morning. He wore a white dress shirt and khaki pants, and he clearly was very nervous. I could see small beads of sweat on his forehead. And I knew he was as afraid as I was that even though he was out on bail, somehow he would be returned to the county jail. A number of hearings were scheduled for the building's several courtrooms that day, but as far as we could tell, Becky and I were the only family members there with defendants. All of us were increasingly tense as we waited for Robin's case to be called.

The tension mounted with each minute that Stephana failed to join us, as she had promised she would. Where was she? She had been highly recommended, but she couldn't help us if she wasn't present.

I put my hand on Robin's back, and I could feel his heart pounding and his fears amplified my own. In an effort to calm both of us down, I told him to imagine he was on a warm and beautiful beach where the waves lapped gently at the sand. And I suggested that he recite silently to himself the childhood prayer I knew he remembered, "Angel of God, My Guardian Dear."

As we sat on the hard bench seats in the courtroom, a woman named Elvie Jacob came over to Robin and shoved some papers at him, telling him to sign them immediately. She said the document was a plea deal that his lawyer Stephana had approved. She was a tall, rangy woman wearing tan work pants and radiating unpleasantness. I grabbed the papers from Robin's hands and told her, "No! He won't be signing anything." She turned and scurried away. It had been only a few seconds, but it was a nightmare scene.

It was late that afternoon before at last Stephana appeared and we were called into the courtroom. Judge Kristen Lucena read the charges against Robin and noted that because he had previously been arrested and convicted on felony charges in California, he was subject to the state's "three strike" repeat-offender sentencing law. The state considered him a "violent criminal" therefore. Hearing the judge describe him that way was absolutely infuriating. Yes, Robin was a drug addict, and by now he was fully fifty years old. But he remained my sweet baby boy, and my heart ached for him.

Robin pleaded not guilty, and Stephana recommended that he request a jury trial because she said that at trial they could use the videos Crystal had filmed to prove their claim that Robin had only acted in self-defense. Despite my growing unease about her poor communication with her client and being constantly late, we thanked her for her help as we left the courthouse. Stephana assured Robin in turn that she would do everything in her power to keep him out of prison. But I had come to believe that the legal system in Butte County, California *wanted* Robin to be guilty. Court officials there believed they were doing God's work, I thought. They wanted to be given credit for putting him behind bars for as long a time as possible. That way, at least their redneck region would be troubled by one less scourge and all the world would be better for it.

Threads of Grace

I was so sick by the time I finally returned to Washington, that I couldn't get out of bed for several days. A nasty virus, plus the awful stress of the events that had occurred while I was in northern California, combined to make me wish I could simply crawl under a rock. During the time I was ill, I didn't get out of my nightgown, didn't eat, didn't read. I talked to as few people as possible on the telephone—and I worried about Robin.

Before I flew home, I had dropped him off at a residential treatment center in Chico called Skyway House. It was a place I had heard about, visited, and thought was the best place for Robin at that moment. It was right there in Chico, small, a facility I could afford, and at least Robin would be out of the woods, have a roof over his head, three meals a day, and be in the company of people whose situation was like his and people whose work it was to help them.

Before Becky and I drove away, Robin walked us to Becky's car and said, "Thank you, Mom, for saving my life again." It touched my heart to hear him say it. And I was surprised that he remembered saying it the first time—back when I dropped him off at the George Washington University metro station when he returned to California following his shooting fourteen years before.

I had hoped in 2008 that coming close to death by shooting would profoundly change him and reset the course he was on, but it had not. The intervening years had seen him lose everything he once had. It seemed unlikely that these most recent events—the fight at the compound on Lovelock Road, his arrest and subhuman treatment in jail, his almost dying a second time, and the very real threat of a long prison sentence—would combine to turn his life around. Still, I hoped they would.

For almost half a century, I had worried about Robin's survival. I observed in horror as he repeatedly made terrible decisions that seemed designed to destroy his life.

But there had been threads of grace along the way—moments when he would do or say something that demonstrated his big heart as well as his cheerful charisma. If I had very little to show for my repeated attempts to help him make a good life for himself, I continued to have hope at least. But hope can be a dangerous thing.

I was finally feeling a bit better when he called from Skyway House. He liked it there, he told me. He liked his therapists and liked his fellow patients—especially a guy he called "Black Adam," a man who wore his hair in dreadlocks and who was roughly Robin's age, both of them older than most of the other patients. It turned out that Stephana was also Adam's lawyer, Robin explained, although he did not tell me what kind of legal trouble had made Adam need a defense lawyer.

It was difficult enough for me to communicate with Stephana when I was present in Butte County but getting her to return my calls and text messages now proved almost impossible once I was home again in Washington. She knew that I was the person paying her fee, which to my mind meant that I was her client as well as Robin. But for whatever reasons, she kept contact with me to the barest minimum. And it worried me because it seemed that if Robin were to avoid prison—and the implied death sentence—it would be because of her efforts as his attorney.

I had been trying to reach Robin's brother Alexander as well, but I had not been successful. I wanted to get Alexander's recommendation for a birthday gift for his daughter Morgan—and to bring him up to date on his brother—but he repeatedly did not respond to the voicemail and text messages I sent. By now, Alexander and his wife made lots of money, lived in a big Georgian house in St. Paul, and had two wonderful children. Each year at Christmas time, they gave friends and family members what I called their "brag book"—a book filled with color photographs of their family's grand adventures from the year just past.

Alexander was my firstborn and I loved him very much. But he and I treated each other carefully. I'm sure he blamed me for many things from his childhood—just as Robin did, especially when Robin was high on something and filled with fury. Alexander no longer raged at me like he once had. But he had become something of a cold fish, and I wished better for him and for my relationship with him.

I was finally feeling almost back to normal again when I next spoke with Robin. He continued to like Skyway, he told me. Dave Deichler, the center's director—whom I had met when I was looking for a Chico-area treatment center that might work for Robin—was an excellent therapist. Robin remained to feel close to Black Adam. He and Adam were Skyway's only "paying customers," Robin told me, adding that all the center's other patients were parolees whose treatment and lodging at Skyway were paid for by the California penal system. They were roughly the same age, and Adam was a "good dude," Robin said. Adam assured him that their lawyer was the best criminal defense lawyer in the region.

Adam had been released from Skyway House for a couple of months by the time Robin was scheduled to appear in court for the second time on July 14 for a trial-readiness conference—to make up for the one at which Stephana failed to appear. She had told Robin she would pick him up at Skyway at 8:00 a.m. and take him to court. She told him she would bring Adam along to keep him company during what she expected to be long hours of waiting at the courthouse. But when neither Stephana nor Adam arrived or even called, a Skyway staff member finally drove Robin to the courthouse in Oroville.

Judge Kristen Lucena grew irate when Stephana did not appear—an offense for which she ultimately fined the lawyer. Robin told the court that he felt he had no choice but to get new representation and asked the court to give him and his new lawyer time to prepare—a request to which the judge agreed. When Robin returned to Skyway, he received a long and scathing text message from Stephana, berating him for "humiliating" her in front of the court and claiming that the judge and deputy district attorney had agreed to the continuance for Robin to find a new lawyer only because "they want me off this case because they are tired of getting their asses kicked."

> You just shot yourself in the other foot because you gave the da's office what they wanted. Don't tell me you don't think we are ready because you have barely got to talk to me. That's a fucking lie. And you know it. You are a grown ass man Robin. You don't need to pull that little boy bullshit and blame your mommy. I know your mom is upset with me because I'm not really communicating with her. I know it's been an issue from the beginning. I at least deserved for you to tell me to my face. Instead of being blindsided like that and embarrassed in front of the court and that sanctimonious bitch of a deputy DA Good luck!

When Robin called to tell me what had taken place in court, and to read Stephana's tirade to me, he confessed that he knew that Adam and Stephana—who was married with three young children—were having an affair. He also knew that she was a heavy user of Oxycontin and other opiates and said he had heard rumors that she often nodded off in court these days, and that her once-stellar reputation was deteriorating quickly.

Stephana was arrested on Friday, July 29, by investigators from the Butte County district attorney's office and charged with harboring Adam Ashford, who was her client and boyfriend. She was also charged with possession of a controlled substance and drug paraphernalia.

The district attorney's office had begun investigating Stephana in June after it learned that she was allegedly hiding Ashford, who was a fugitive on several federal felony arrest warrants. Ashford had been on probation—and in residence at Skyway, where he became Robin's friend—but he failed to appear for his own court date on May 11. Stephana, who appeared in court on his behalf, said she did not know where her client was nor why he had failed to appear. With that, a superior court judge issued a "no bail" warrant for Black Adam's arrest.

Ashford was a felon on probation following several convictions, including possession of drugs while armed with a firearm, assault with a deadly weapon, and felony evading the police. Stephana had represented Ashford in those cases. She was with him when he was arrested on June 24 and held without bail, and it was following his arrest that the investigation of her intensified.

Soon after she was arrested late in July, an Oroville woman who was a former client claimed Stephana had forced her to pay $2,500 to Ashford, telling her that he was a "private investigator" at work on her case. Similarly, Stephana had come to the Airbnb we were renting in Chico when I was there in February of that year. She was accompanied by one of her young sons and was wearing a heavy winter coat and bedroom slippers. She was clearly falling apart. She told me she needed $750 *right now* because she had to hire an investigator to help with Robin's case. I still don't know whether the money I gave her went to

Ashford or to buy drugs or something else, but I do know that she never hired an investigator on Robin's behalf.

The DA's office alleged that Stephana had allowed Ashford to live in her law office in Chico for the two months leading up to his arrest, during which time she continued to claim that she didn't know his whereabouts. For now, at least, Stephana—who had been released from Butte County jail on bond—retained her license to practice law. Because she had dropped the ball so thoroughly in Robin's case, and because of her professional shortcomings, he was now forced to find a new lawyer.

As summer gave way to fall, I continued to be terrified that Robin would be sent to prison, where his chances for survival would be so small. But something now was unmistakably different about him. For the first time ever, he seemed truly determined to set his life on a better course. Relapsing was commonplace among addicts, of course, so I would be foolish to get my hopes up. Robin could fall massively off the wagon any day—and that would be that. He wrote in a text, "Things are looking up. But I've got a lot of wreckage to deal with. No surprise there." Those words were direct, and they implicitly expressed his understanding that he was responsible for his predicaments. Not anyone else.

I was eighty-seven years old. My health was not so good, and any travel—let alone those cross-country trips to California—would be very difficult for me. My pulmonologist reported that my lungs had been severely impacted by the stress. As I had for decades, I spent much of my time worrying about Robin and I also reflected on old memories, like the time when he was a little boy and contracted spinal meningitis.

John had taken the little boys to visit his mother at her summer place in York, Maine. He called to tell me Robin was very ill, cautioning me that the doctors told him he might not last the night. When I finally got there several hours later, I found him sleeping curled up in a crib in the hospital. He recovered; and we had been fortunate that John got Robin medical attention as quickly as he did, but the meningitis had lasting effects.

When he was in elementary school, his teachers said he had difficulty concentrating and struggled with fine motor skills like handwriting or cutting designs with scissors. When he was challenged by a task, he would stop and say, "I can't do this," rather than keep on trying. In 1986, when he was twelve, psychiatrist Peter Mueller, an old friend from the NIH, who now lived and worked in Princeton, New Jersey, tested Robin and found evidence of abnormal electrical activity in his frontal lobe. Peter was convinced that the meningitis Robin had suffered in Maine was the root of his attention deficit, hyperactivity and impulsivity, and his occasional migraines.

Was it the cause of his life of turmoil and drug addiction as well? It might have played a part—it must have had *some* sort of role, I believed. But Robin's brother had been a heroin addict, too. And he had never had encephalitis. The boys were brought up in the same household. The DNA they received from their father and me was identical, and Alexander had ultimately made a success of his life. Robin, on the other hand, seemed to have thrown his many gifts away, opting for adventure that, over time, became nothing more than chaos.

Had I been a bad mother? Was I to blame? Like virtually every other parent, I had done the best I could. But *I* was the parent who'd had the role of disciplinarian. It fell to me to explain to the boys that they could not go skiing, for example, because it was too costly, and because we could not risk one of them getting injured because we didn't have health insurance.

Was it John? It seemed to me that both boys had inherited their father's sense of entitlement. Both believed that they should be handed all the good things life had on offer—just as their father did—but surely that was not the reason Robin was now over fifty and an aging addict.

Because I was paying for Robin's defense, I played a significant part in the search for a lawyer to replace Stephana. I would get up at the crack of dawn and scour the Internet and make long lists, trying to find someone who would take the case—and I ultimately interviewed ten or more defense attorneys. Several lawyers I spoke with by telephone from Washington declined to take the case, citing conflict of interest or some other reason. Some gave me no reason at all; they simply said no. Then finally, Saul Henson said maybe. Based in Chico, Henson was solely a criminal defense attorney, and he was someone who was well-known in the community. I learned that his father had been in jail when he was young—and I presumed that he had chosen his career, at least in part, to help others avoid his father's fate.

When we first talked on the phone, he was crisp and clear—and emphatic about his fees. Robin later reported to me that Henson was perhaps ten years younger than he was, big, "hippyish," handsome, bearded, and self-possessed. He paid close attention to every detail Robin shared with him about his legal circumstances before he formally agreed to take the case. It wouldn't be easy to get the charges dropped, he cautioned, and he raised the possibility that perhaps getting Robin accepted into California's drug-court program was something to which the court would agree.

California drug courts offer defendants charged with nonviolent drug offenses a chance to resolve their cases without going through the normal criminal-justice system. When a drug offender successfully completes a drug treatment program, he can simply get his criminal charges dismissed. Instead of going to prison, Robin could potentially enter closely monitored substance abuse treatment. Henson cautioned that Robin was charged with *violent* offenses, so getting him accepted into drug court was far from given.

And there was another serious issue. If Robin went to drug court ordered treatment, he would have to stay in Butte County. And he was desperate to leave there. The region around Chico held nightmarish memories for him, and he would face lots of temptations if he was forced to stay. He said he preferred to risk a jury trial. If he was found not guilty, he could make a permanent move to Oakland—the city where he wanted to live. It was a huge gamble, but he said he preferred a drug trial to agreeing to drug court and being captive to Butte County, where he believed he might be returned to jail unfairly and "stomped out" again.

I had visited Robin in Oakland and had seen enough of his life at the warehouse to be afraid that he would find the ready availability of hard drugs there hard to resist. Yet for Robin—born a city boy, of course—perhaps Oakland simply, and finally, held real appeal for him over the sordid life he had lived for decades in far more redneck, rural northern California.

In late September, I sent an email reply to a message I'd had from my niece, a physician who cared deeply about Robin:

I had a talk with lawyer Saul Henson, and it seems the latest plan is for a trial on December 12. That's the date but he and Robin are still discussing drug court. Saul prefers drug court but that would all take place in Chico. Robin has very bad memories of Chico—naturally. And he's trying to get housing and establish a life in Oakland. It's up to them to work out a course of action. My tentative plan is to go to Chico. Lots of variables there, of course. My basic intention is to support Robin in what I see as a brave and lonely journey. I am in awe of how far he has come. I dread a relapse. If he thinks it matters to have me there, I will go. I do, in general, agree in preferring drug court to trial but this the decision is not mine to make. Robin has made a huge and brave effort to move out of the drug world. It is fraught with dangers and difficulties. Success is not assured. In addition to trying to escape addiction, he faces many difficulties, medical housing, transportation, lack of friends or a support system—and more. He is working as hard as he can on all these issues. He expresses his gratitude to me. Sadly, I think I am his safety net and reliable supporter. In both cases—the only one. I know you prefer I not take the risk of travel. I understand that. But as old as I am, time is short either way. It's important to me to do whatever I can to help Robin stay on his course. We are nearing a time of serious stress—legal, recovery related, and the loneliness of Christmas. I think it would ease his way to have me there—to literally stand by him. That's all a long way of saying—it's not set in stone and many things could change my thinking—but right now my idea is to go to California and probably stay through Christmas.

For decades it would have been unimaginable for me to write that positively about Robin—impossible because I had never before seen him that determined to turn his life around. I had been deeply pessimistic about his ever escaping the drug world. It often seemed that drugs and guns and living out of control were the only life he knew, the only one he wanted.

It's hard to pinpoint precisely when—and why—sometime in the latter half of 2022 Robin began to approach his life in a new and self-nurturing way. I was hospitalized for five days in April with COPD complications, and during that time he didn't call, which worried me because living—for both of us—had become a tricky business.

By October, however, Robin was reaching out to me several times a week. He seemed to enjoy our telephone calls and, for the first time since he was a small boy, he expressed that he appreciated and needed me. He told me he had been impressed by the people he had met in hospitals over the years and by their commitment to helping others. He said he imagined that he could become some kind of medical assistant—a good one—and I replied that, yes, I agreed he would find that work fulfilling.

In Oakland, he was living in the back of his van—one that wasn't drivable, even if he had money for gas. He went to Alcoholics Anonymous and Narcotics Anonymous meetings several times a week and reported that the support he found from others like him who were determined to set their lives straight was important to him.

He spent his days focused simply on the basics of daily life—finding places where he could use the bathroom and wash himself, taking buses to buy food and bring it back to his van, "cooking" it on a kerosene camping stove, going to meetings and keeping doctor and dentist appointments.

Robin stayed in contact with his longtime girlfriend Crystal—also an addict, of course—and she was often with him in Oakland. Although I doubted that they were deeply in love, they cared about each other and cared for each other as well. Crystal was someone who had virtually no education, but she was smart, and she knew how to get things done. Although their shared addiction made them poor influences on each other, I was nonetheless proud that Robin had not simply abandoned Crystal. And I appreciated the fact that she was one of the few people in California who truly cared about his well-being.

Robin's lifelong friend Chris Kelly—who almost miraculously had escaped addiction himself—grew legal marijuana near Calistoga, California. Chris continued to hold Robin in a kind of awe, and although he acknowledged to me that Robin had made many bad decisions over the years when we frequently spoke by phone, he would never give up on his friend.

Robin was determined to make amends with Paul Schaechter, the friend from Washington, who had migrated to northern California. Someone Robin had known almost as long as Chris, Paul had had his fill of Robin some years before. He was afraid of him and wanted no contact with him. But Robin said reconnecting with Paul was now important to him.

I continued to try my best not to get my hopes up, but I also wanted to support Robin's brave new attempt to save his own life. I wrote to him that fall, reminding him of my mother, and of both boys when they were young, and the love that sustained us all despite dangers both large and small.

> You probably don't remember my mother. You were just a little boy. We would an often go to her apartment on Connecticut Avenue for tea. Over my objection, she served you and Alexander with delicate fine china. She never worried that it might break, and she told me to go out and leave her to manage the tea in her own way. So, I did. . . . Somehow at her place nothing ever spilled, and nothing was ever broken. And a cross word was never spoken. That was long ago, and our lives have taken many twists and turns since then. But what has always been constant is love. She loved you dearly—and so do I. You have had big times—exciting, productive, lucrative and awful dark times, too. Now you are making a huge turn in your life. And I want you to know how much I admire your courage to make the change—your bravery in this—to quit drugs and start a whole new life. There's little I can do to help you. But whatever I can do, I will do. I love you. I'm proud of you and I stand with you.

I hoped that Alexander would take an interest in his brother. I hoped he would support Robin's new determination to make himself a new life. But Alexander had never been close to his brother and that seemed unlikely to change. Based on his years in the recovery business, I thought Alexander's insight into Robin's circumstances would be helpful, but I was troubled by what I heard. When Robin reached out to his brother by phone and directly asked for help, apparently Alexander's response was cool. I wasn't part of their conversation, but Robin's account of it concerned me. "What Robin wanted from you," I wrote to Alexander, "was the comfort of you loving him, or just caring about him, and maybe willing to use your knowledge of addiction to help him."

"Robin is exactly where he wants to be," Alexander responded. He was the expert, but I certainly didn't agree with him. "Maybe Robin and I should give up wishing you loved us both and quit bothering you," I wrote.

On the face of things, Alexander had everything anyone could ask of life. But I was unhappy that he showed so little affection for me or his brother. When we spoke three or four times a year, I would hear about wonderful holidays in grand places, about his kids' achievements, and the successes he and Leslie had made. But he never asked about me—my activities, my health, or my encounters with people we both knew. And he was always utterly dismissive of Robin. I didn't know how to account for such disinterest.

I knew Alexander suffered chronic neck pain. Nothing had ever helped, and even the Cleveland Clinic could not find the cause. It might be that the pain was psychic, not physical. Alexander worked hard to block much of his life experience from his memory, and it deeply saddened me that he also repressed the fact that he had a brother who was a junkie.

But in that same October, I was surprised one day to have a call from Alexander, who said that he and his family planned to come to Washington in November and spend time with me. I was pleased and told him that would be wonderful. I had not seen his two young children for five years, and, of course, I would love to have them come visit. Although I cautioned him that because of my breathing problems and the fact that I was on oxygen, I couldn't join them in exploring the city's museums.

Sally, the boy's stepmother once joked that it wasn't that Alexander and his family didn't like us—it was the fact that they didn't know we were alive. So, it was very unexpected to receive that call and to see Alexander and family back in the city where he grew up.

During the days they spent in Washington in November, our time together went smoothly. The children knew who I was, of course, but it's almost impossible to truly love someone with whom you've never spent time. Leslie was lovely. She was very clearly at ease with herself and comfortable with her new position as CEO of the healthcare company. But I did not feel as close to her as I had been to several of the women in my sons' earlier lives.

Talking with Alexander was like conversing with someone you have met but don't really know. Quite literally, our conversations were about the day's weather, a column in the *Washington Post* we both had read, a magazine that was lying on my coffee table—nothing of any substance. When I tried to tell him something about Robin at lunch one day, he cut me off sharply saying, "I don't want to talk about that." So, we didn't.

Robin's trial, scheduled for December 12, was postponed until March because Will Tiplick, the man who had attacked him with a broken bottle, no longer lived in California and had to be subpoenaed to attend the trial and testify. So, Robin could travel at Christmastime, and, as he often had over the years, he came to Washington for the holiday.

He didn't stay long, but he was with me on Christmas Day when Alexander called. I put my phone on speaker, passed it to Robin, and I listened as my two sons had a very good and connective conversation—one that seemed to me to be the best kind of gift I could have received. Alexander was warm, and I know Robin appreciated the way his brother engaged with him. Alexander seemed to recognize in his brother's voice the same thing that I both heard and observed. There was something *different* about Robin now. He was alert and at ease in ways he hadn't been in decades.

I was delighted when Alexander asked his brother if he would like to come to St. Paul to visit. Robin quickly responded that he would like that very much. Alexander promised to send him an airline ticket in the spring—when the Minnesota weather would be much more inviting. And it would make sense for Robin to come visit only once his legal woes were behind him.

Alexander's implied optimism was perfect for Christmas day. But all of us knew that come spring, it was possible that Robin would be serving time in a California prison somewhere rather than traveling to St. Paul. Robin's future remained unclear. His lawyer Saul Henson continued to think that getting Robin accepted into Butte County's drug court was the safest option for him. But Robin was afraid of that possibility. Little by little, he was creating a new life in Oakland. If drug court would keep him out of prison but demand that he live in the Chico area during the coming years, he was afraid his new life would be all but impossible to maintain.

When Robin was with me in Washington at Christmas, I did not tell him that his son Matthew was engaged to be married. Matthew had been very clear with me that his father would not be invited to his wedding. Matthew was going to marry a lovely Trinidadian woman he had met at the University of Delaware and Matthew simply wouldn't risk his father spoiling the very special occasion.

I knew hearing that he would be excluded from an event that should have been one of the highlights of Robin's life would have hurt his heart. And little by little, his heart was mending. For now, I chose—rightly or wrongly—to say nothing about Matthew's life or his bride, focusing instead on the kinds of simple support I thought might be helpful as his trial approached early in 2023.

Robin continued to believe that the risk of being convicted at trial of the charges stemming from the June 2021 violence was preferable to accepting the demands of drug court and being required to stay in Butte County for two or three years. His attorney continued to disagree. But Henson did understand that a prison sentence was more likely to lead to Robin's injury or death than drug court. And he made it clear that he would do his best to keep his client out of prison.

Robin and Henson communicated well as far as I could tell from nearly three thousand miles away. They respected each other and made a good team, although Henson remained cool toward me. He told Robin that he had had bad experiences with family members—mothers in particular—who interfered with and disrupted his cases. I was determined not to get in the way, but it was maddening to do nothing but worry. One day in January, out of a sense of helplessness and rage, I typed out a summary of the incident and the circumstances in court and the county jail that had followed. "Punishments are held to be just to the extent that they take into account relevant criteria such as the seriousness of the crime and the *intent* of the criminal," I wrote, citing the Markkula Center for Applied Ethics. "To find the truth you must listen to both sides of the story."

THE INTENT:

Two men seen threatening Robin.

Robin's intent: self-defense.

Feared for his life and girlfriend Crystal.

Tiplick and Hogan's INTENT: to kill Robin.

Robin came out of cabin 6 carrying small handgun for self-defense.

Robin fired two shots into abandoned trailer to frighten Tiplick and Hogan.

Robin right-handed, moved gun to left hand, dangling toward the ground.

Tiplick attacked Robin with a glass half-gallon Jim Beam bottle.

Struck Robin's hand causing accidental discharge of gun.

Tiplick told police he did not think Robin intended to harm him.

Tiplick later found passed-out drunk, wet himself, lying in driveway.

The charges:

Tiplick did not file charges.

Charges filed against Robin:

Discharging firearm that could cause injury or death. Gross negligence.

Shooting at inhabited dwelling.

Assault with firearm on William Murray Tiplick.

Judge labeled robbing a "dangerous and violent criminal."

Judge announced, "suspect guilt—held to cause."

JAIL:

Robin in pod with approximately 60 men.

Severely beaten and "stomped out" like George Floyd.

Near death, taken to Oroville Hospital for four days' treatment and recovery.

Dr. Patel: Robin had COVID, hepatitis, pneumonia, and infection on hugely swollen foot.

After treatment, Robin returned to Oroville jail.

Lawyer Stephana Femino found Robin in jail shackled to steal bunk, lying in own waste, in coma.

No sweater, no blanket, had not been able to use toilet because shackled.

Released on bail.

Physical condition on release:

Dehydrated.

Extreme weight loss.

Disoriented.

Barely able to stand.

DAMAGES: None.

No harm to Tiplick or any other person.

Two bullet holes in derelict trailer.

ROBIN:

Not tried.

Not convicted.

Not sentenced.

<u>Severely punished.</u>

<u>Twice left for dead.</u>

Robin suffered physical and emotional damage.

Robin's family suffered emotional strain and financial strain from expenses including travel, bail, legal and medical.

"There is a delicate line between the pursuit of justice and indulging urge for retribution.," my summary concluded. "Is this justice?"

Robin would turn fifty-two in the spring and throughout virtually all his life I had worried about him—his decisions, the company he kept, the chances for his survival. Although he had often lashed out at me during that half century, I was also terribly aware that he really had no one else in the world that he could rely on. There was no one else he *knew* would be there if he asked. But if you're in your fifties and the only person to whom you can turn is your elderly mother, that's pathetic, isn't it? I wanted him to have so much more than only me in his life, but I had to be realistic, too, and I was all he had.

Early in 2023, I was both optimistic that at last Robin was ready to turn his life around and frightened that the violent incident in the encampment north of Magalia would end up taking his life just as he finally was ready to claim it and change it for the better. And I wasn't sure if I could be any more help—or if I had ever been helpful. The physical challenges of traveling in my questionable health, the horrors I witnessed after Robin was left for dead in the Butte County jail, and the awful stress of attempting to find some justice for him had come close to killing me. When I had gone to California ten months before, my *spirit* was willing to return to California. I was open to jumping on a flight in an instant if I was needed. But I had to be sensible, and I dreaded having to fly west again.

And Robin was undeniably different now. He truly wanted to escape his downward-spiraling life. It horrified me to think that he might come *this* close to escaping addiction and violence, only to be unfairly jailed—where, I was sure, he would die. I had spent countless hours on the telephone from my apartment in Washington, attempting to find a defense lawyer who would replace the accused felon and drug-addicted Stephana Femino.

When I spoke with Robin by phone, I often told him how proud I was of him. I told him I believed in him. I even tried to teach my middle-aged son how to create a simple budget with an allotment of $250 a week, so that the monthly $1,000 disability income his foot injury provided could stretch to the end of each month.

Writing that summary of the Magalia incident made it ever more clear in my mind that Robin had not been treated fairly beginning that day in June 2021 when he stepped onto the porch of the cabin in the woods and fired two warning shots into a nearby abandoned trailer. But California's shockingly bad legal and penal systems had come very close to killing my son in the intervening months, and I had to say *something*, do *something*. So, I emailed my summary to Saul Henson. Reading what I had written seemed to improve his opinion of me and the role I was playing in Robin's life, in addition to being the person who paid his fees.

In response to my query, Henson said yes, I could send the summary to the judge, the Butte County sheriff's office, the district attorney's office, and Butte County Superior Court, but getting anyone to actually read it and pay attention to it would be unlikely. He said he wished that weren't the case, but it was. He wanted me to consider that getting Robin accepted into drug court in lieu of going to trial and possibly jail would be a huge victory—and it was an outcome he truly believed was possible. He said two or three years in drug court in Chico likely would "inspire" Robin. But in my sometimes very blunt way, I told him that was ridiculous.

Robin *hated* Chico and Butte County. That was where his life had taken its most desperate turn. And it was the place where a system supposedly dedicated to his innocence until he was proven guilty, had come crashing down on him—leaving him comatose and chained to a steel slab as he lay in his own waste. Nothing—not even death—would be worse than jail. And the idea of being forced to live in the Chico area as he attempted to create a sober life was intolerable. He would pass each day in fear that *somehow* he could be snatched off the street and returned to jail where he would be beaten again. When I shared his perspective with Henson, he at last seemed to understand.

Beginning with that conversation, Henson's goals for the case suddenly, but very substantially changed. Instead of working toward a resolution of the charges that would inspire Robin to fundamentally change his life, he now began to consider another possibility. He agreed that a jail sentence—even one that demanded only six months or so in the county jail rather than a long stretch in a state penitentiary—had to be considered off the table. Given Robin's always-infected foot, his seizures, and his addictions, of course, even the shortest time in incarceration would be a death sentence. He finally understood that.

But maybe, *maybe* there was another option. If Robin were paroled for a year or two, and if he were squeaky clean and a model citizen during that time, the shooting charges would be expunged from his record. If paroled, Henson said, the court likely would allow Robin to live in Oakland and serve his parole time there. Parole, it now seemed to Henson, Robin, and me was the path forward that would give him a chance. Its success was far from assured, but it was an opportunity Robin deserved.

In Oakland. Robin continued to live in his inoperable van. He was one of an estimated 116,000 Californians who were homeless in 2023. Fully eighteen percent of the entire U.S. population was unsheltered as well, and the national crisis was deepening every day. Robin fully appreciated by now that he could do nothing more than live one day at a time. His focus had to be keeping himself relatively safe, looking after his basic food, bathing, and toileting needs, keeping his foot in the healthiest condition he could, and meticulously attending his medical and other appointments and the Alcoholics Anonymous and Narcotics Anonymous meetings where, he reported to me, he was learning a great deal about himself and about how to deal with his challenges.

It was at AA meetings, too, where Robin was beginning to create friendly relationships with others who were similarly attempting to climb their way out of addiction—men who were doctors, truck drivers, businesspeople, and laborers who shared a common desire to transform their despair into real hope. Robin and many of the men he met were making their first real friends in years—or were beginning at least to imagine that friendships could once again be important parts of their lives. And Robin told me he could now imagine making friends with at least a few of them in ways that would last.

Sometimes he still saw his girlfriend Crystal. I worried that when she came to Oakland, the pressure for him to join her in taking drugs would overwhelm him, but I also appreciated that caring about Crystal allowed him to express something of his inherent love for people. It was my opinion that there was little chance for Crystal to become sober, and in our conversations I tried to remind Robin that he could not change Crystal's life in the way that he could his own. He wanted me to know that he was doing his best to arrange for Crystal to get a job of sorts, looking after a friend of theirs who had cancer and needed assistance. Robin was beginning to think again about ways in which he could help others.

Although his legal jeopardy continued, there was much to be hopeful about as winter warmed in the spring. But it was not an easy time. I have to be on oxygen twenty-four hours a day now. My stamina was limited, and I had a bad mammogram that meant I would need surgery, but these things seemed trifling in comparison to the physical challenges of the two weeks I had spent in Chico in 2022. Throughout my life, I had been lucky to have good friends—men and women, some in the financial world, of course, and a number of physicians and scientists at the National Institutes of Health. Some friends who were especially important to me had died, and I increasingly felt alone, just as Robin did.

My California nieces—whom I loved and who had always been supportive of my determination to do what I could for Robin—seemed to have had enough. He was nothing more than a degenerate druggie, and experiences of every sort in their own lives convinced them that Robin was beyond being helped, and that I was being foolish. And I increasingly found myself uninterested in talking to friends or family members about Robin's life.

It seemed nothing short of tragic to me that my son who was highly successful would *never* speak with me about his drug addicted brother. When Alexander and his wife came to Washington for business meetings that May, he and I had a single lunch. Like always, it felt like I was dining with acquaintances, and when I mentioned Robin, Alexander stiffened and rather angrily said, "I don't want to talk about that," just as he had before. Neither did we talk about my health or anything else of any substance. When Mother's Day arrived not long thereafter, an enormous potted orchid was delivered to my apartment. I would have far preferred a small bunch of flowers or a real conversation with Alexander.

The previous Christmas, I had been present when Alexander told Robin by telephone that he looked forward to hosting him in Minnesota before long, but Alexander had never raised the possibility again, and I had to presume that he no longer wanted Robin to visit— if, in fact, if he ever truly had.

I was beginning to get excited. In June, I would attend Matthew's wedding, and it would be a wonderful event. Matthew's step-grandmother Sally and I would both be in attendance, but neither Matthew's father nor his uncle were invited—and Robin, of course, knew nothing at all about the wedding. When we were imagining a bright future for Robin during one of our conversations, I told him that I believed he could reestablish his relationship with his son someday. But I cautioned him that he shouldn't even try until he had held a job and been truly sober for a year or two. He needed to be able to point to that success with Matthew and to say, in effect, "I'm different now. I truly am. And you can see that. But I remain your dad and I want you in my life."

"Choose Chico" is the tagline of a program created by the small city to tout the myriad reasons anyone and everyone would want to live, work, and play in "California's largest city, north of the capital city Sacramento." Chico is home to about a hundred thousand people and roughly twice that number live in Butte County. It's an area that boasts a state university, balmy weather, and friendly, if largely conservative, people. There are some good restaurants. But it's also a hotbed of anti-vaccination sentiment—a reaction to COVID and the unconscionable lies about the vaccine that, as someone who believes in science and medicine, I simply cannot understand.

Robin's lawyer Saul Henson was one of those Butte County residents who were opposed to COVID vaccination, although he had already contracted the virus twice. And he, like many of his neighbors was also highly suspicious of doctors—so much so that he didn't have one and would go to the local emergency room when he needed some sort of medical record to prove to the court that he was ill and could not attend.

But Robin thought highly of Henson, and I respected that. Robin was far more familiar with northern California's particular kind of leave-us-alone conservatism than I was. I had strongly negative opinions about the public safety and legal systems in Butte County as well. But when Henson began to focus his efforts on keeping Robin out of jail and getting him out of Chico for good by securing parole, I kept my misgivings to myself. In conversations with me, Henson swore that Robin had become a friend and far more than simply another client to him. And he said he looked forward to visiting him in the Bay Area in the future—at a time when the Magalia nightmare had become history and Robin was living a new life.

In January 2021, California Governor Gavin Newsom signed AB1950 into law, new legislation designed to reduce the number of inmates in prison in the state and lower the enormous cost of operating jails and prisons. The new law also reduced the term of parole convictions for misdemeanors from three years to one year, and for felonies from five years to two years. In practice, the legislation was already sparing large numbers of criminal defendants from prison time, and it appeared its existence might well keep Robin out of jail as well.

On March 15, 2023, Robin took a long and uncomfortable bus ride from Oakland to Chico, spent the night in an inexpensive motel, then appeared in court the following day with Saul Henson by his side. During the course of the hearing, Judge Kristen Lucena dismissed three of the four pending charges against Robin—assault with a firearm, use of a firearm in the commission of a felony and shooting at an occupied motor vehicle or house. The judge did *not* dismiss the charge of using a firearm with gross negligence.

Robin formally waived his right to a jury trial, and the judge canceled a trial that had been scheduled for late March, then set a sentencing date for the remaining charge in May. Everything appeared to be falling into place for Robin to be convicted on the gross negligence charge, then to be sentenced to probation. Henson enthusiastically told me that Robin had conducted himself very well in court, and said he was optimistic that a probation conviction was on the way. But, he said, "nothing is ever certain until it occurs in open court," and Robin returned to Oakland, his fate still uncertain.

Eight weeks later, Robin traveled to Chico by bus again, this time in possession of several letters from his physicians—each one affirming that Robin was working hard to keep himself healthy and to end his years of addictions.

At his sentencing hearing on May 11, 2023, Judge Lucena convicted Robin of the gross negligence charge and sentenced him to two years of probation. At last, the horror was over it appeared until the deputy district attorney told the judge that because Robin's myriad illnesses more than a year before had necessitated his transfer from county jail to the hospital, he should still be required by the court to spend eight days behind bars in addition to the probation conviction.

I knew from watching her in court more than a year before that the deputy DA was one of those professional women who is always perfectly turned out in plain skirt and jacket, wearing no jewelry, her hair in conservative precision—the kind of person whose goal is always to appear utterly in control of herself and, by extension, in control of every matter to which she attends. Almost certainly, her goal was to further punish Robin, to seek the maximum possible penalty for him—exactly as she did in every case.

On behalf of his client, Henson raised the possibility of Robin serving the eight days under house arrest in a Chico motel. He would wear an ankle bracelet, his food would be brought in, and under no circumstances would he be allowed to leave. The judge chose not to rule immediately on the DA's motion, and she took both attorneys' statements under advisement. She would issue a ruling soon, she said from the bench. And that was that.

I was outraged when I received the news. Robin had come very close to dying in the Butte County jail twice before. Who could believe that he would not suffer a similar fate if he was forced to return to jail? Was this justice? Although the house-arrest option would not result in Robin's death, the cost would likely be $2,000 or so, an amount I would pay if I had to, but would *that* be justice?

On June 16, Judge Lucena finally ruled that Robin would be jailed for eight days, and he was immediately transferred to the Butte County jail in Oroville. For more than a week, I was terrified that I would receive a telephone call with very bad news, but mercifully, that call never came. Robin survived the eight days without a horrible incident—although he left the jail twenty pounds lighter than before—then he returned to Oakland. His parole plan was officially transferred from Butte County to Alameda County, where he is now, and I know he hopes never to see Chico again.

It might have been a celebratory moment but I—and all of us—had endured enough by now that there didn't seem to be anything to celebrate. Even misery, when it's been with us for decades, has its own kind of comfort. Things were no longer miserable, but they had not instantly been transformed into a comfortable new life. For the foreseeable future, Robin would continue to live in his van and would, day by day, attempt to create a life that was brand new for him. I was enormously proud of him. But I was also exhausted and more than a little worn by the decades of the slow grinding down of hope.

This time was going to be different, I wanted to believe, but who could know? Whether it happened before my days were done or after I was gone, I dreamed that both my sons could finally slay the personal dragons that beset them. In their separate ways, I dreamed that both Robin and Alexander would learn at last that nothing matters in the end except love—the love of family and dear friends that give life meaning.

The sky had been dark for a very long time, but at last a bit of light had begun to burn through. At last, the future held something like promise. I wanted nothing more for Robin as the days and months unfolded than for him to thrive. And I wanted to attend his son's wedding as a kind of stand-in for him, filled on that day of celebration with every good wish for all of us in this family that has shaped my long life.

About the Author

Eliza Richards is a retired financial advisor in Washington, D.C., USA, where she has lived many years. Her father had a distinguished, decades-long career in the U.S. Army and she is a direct descendant of Francis Scott Key, who composed "The Star-Spangled Banner." She is the mother of two sons and has three grandchildren.

Made in the USA
Coppell, TX
16 October 2024